The Singularitys Lament

Unveiling the Future of Human Machine Integration and Its Impact on Society

Whitney Adams

Chapter 1: The Dawn of the Singularity

Introduction to the Concept of Singularity

The concept of singularity stands as a pivotal point in the narrative of human evolution, a juncture where the boundaries between human and machine become increasingly blurred. It's a notion that has captured the imagination of futurists, technologists, and philosophers alike. At its core, singularity refers to a hypothetical future moment when technological growth becomes uncontrollable and irreversible, resulting in unforeseeable changes to human civilization. This transformation is primarily driven by advancements in artificial intelligence and machine learning, where machines surpass human intelligence and capability.

The roots of singularity trace back to the mid-20th century, a period marked by rapid technological advancements. Visionaries like mathematician John von Neumann and science fiction writer Vernor Vinge speculated about an impending epoch where machines would rival, if not exceed, human cognitive abilities. These early musings laid the foundation for the modern understanding of singularity, which gained further traction with the works of renowned futurist Ray Kurzweil, who predicted that singularity would occur by the mid-21st century.

At the heart of singularity lies the exponential growth of technology. Unlike linear progress, where advancements occur at a steady pace, exponential growth implies that each technological breakthrough accelerates the pace of future innovations. This is vividly exemplified by Moore's Law, which posits that the number of transistors on a microchip doubles approximately every two years, leading to the rapid escalation of computing power. As technology advances exponentially, the timeline for achieving singularity appears increasingly plausible.

Understanding the singularity requires an exploration of the interplay between artificial intelligence and human cognition. The trajectory of AI development has been characterized by milestones such as the creation of neural networks, deep learning algorithms, and natural language processing. These advancements have enabled machines to perform tasks that were once deemed the exclusive domain of human intelligence, from language translation to complex problem-solving. As AI systems continue to evolve, the potential for machines to develop self-awareness and autonomous decision-making grows, inching us closer to the singularity.

However, the journey toward singularity is fraught with challenges and uncertainties. The prospect of machines surpassing human intelligence raises profound philosophical and ethical questions. What does it mean for humans to coexist with entities that possess superior cognitive abilities? How do we ensure that machines align with human values and priorities? The singularity not only promises unprecedented technological capabilities but also demands a reexamination of the very essence of humanity.

The singularity also invites us to reconsider the nature of consciousness. Traditionally, consciousness has been viewed as an inherently human trait, rooted in subjective experiences and self-awareness. The potential for machines to achieve consciousness challenges this notion, prompting debates about the definition and scope of consciousness itself. If machines can attain a level of awareness akin to human consciousness, it raises questions about their rights, responsibilities, and place in society.

As we inch closer to the singularity, the role of human-machine integration becomes increasingly significant. This integration is not merely about enhancing human capabilities but also about redefining the relationship between humans and technology. From wearable devices that monitor health metrics to brain-computer interfaces that enable direct communication between the brain and external devices, the convergence of human and machine is already underway. These technologies hold the promise of augmenting human potential, allowing us to transcend our biological limitations.

Yet, the integration of technology into the human experience is not without its complexities. It necessitates a careful balancing act between innovation and caution, ensuring that technological advancements are harnessed for the greater good. This involves addressing concerns related to privacy, security, and ethical considerations. As technology becomes more intertwined with our lives, the need for robust frameworks and guidelines becomes paramount to navigate the myriad challenges that arise in this new era of human-machine coexistence.

The singularity is not a distant dream but an impending reality that demands our attention and preparation. It challenges us to rethink our understanding of intelligence, consciousness, and the human experience. As we stand on the brink of this transformative moment, we must engage in meaningful dialogue and collaboration across disciplines to shape a future where technology serves humanity, rather than the other way around.

The path to singularity is not predetermined, but rather a journey shaped by human choices and actions. It is an opportunity to redefine what it means to be human in an age where machines become our intellectual counterparts. By embracing the possibilities and addressing the challenges, we can pave the way for a harmonious coexistence between humans and machines, unlocking new potentials and fostering a future where technology enhances the human experience in profound and meaningful ways.

Historical Perspectives on Human Machine Evolution

The story of human-machine evolution is a testament to humanity's relentless quest for advancement, driven by curiosity and necessity. It is a tale that unfolds over centuries, a narrative that weaves together the ingenuity of human innovation with the ever-changing landscape of technology. This journey began long before the age of digital technology, rooted in the mechanical inventions that laid the groundwork for the machines we rely on today.

In ancient times, humans sought to extend their physical capabilities through simple machines. The wheel, lever, and pulley are among the earliest examples of human ingenuity, allowing our ancestors to manipulate their environment with greater efficiency. These rudimentary tools were the precursors to more complex machines, setting the stage for the technological advancements of future generations. As societies became more sophisticated, so too did their machines, evolving from basic implements to intricate devices that transformed daily life.

The Industrial Revolution marked a significant turning point in the history of human-machine evolution. It was a period of unprecedented change, characterized by the rise of mechanization and the birth of modern industry. Steam engines, textile machinery, and iron production were at the forefront of this transformation, revolutionizing manufacturing processes and reshaping economies. The factory system emerged, with machines becoming integral to production lines, increasing efficiency and output. This era not only altered the nature of work but also redefined the relationship between humans and machines, as mechanization began to permeate various aspects of society.

As the 19th century gave way to the 20th, technological innovation continued to accelerate. The invention of electricity and the development of the internal combustion engine ushered in a new era of possibilities. Electricity powered new inventions, from light bulbs to telegraphs, while automobiles and airplanes expanded the horizons of transportation.

These advancements were catalysts for societal change, leading to urbanization and the rise of consumer culture. Machines became symbols of progress and modernity, embedding themselves into the fabric of everyday life.

World War II served as another pivotal moment, driving rapid advancements in technology and engineering. The war effort necessitated the development of new machines, from radar systems to jet engines, which would later find peacetime applications. The post-war period saw the rise of computers, initially developed for military use, which gradually transitioned into civilian life. The electronic computer, a marvel of human ingenuity, marked the beginning of the digital age, forever altering the trajectory of human-machine evolution.

The latter half of the 20th century witnessed a technological renaissance, as computers evolved from room-sized behemoths to personal devices, becoming increasingly accessible to the general public. The microprocessor, a remarkable feat of engineering, paved the way for the proliferation of personal computers and the dawn of the information age. The internet emerged as a global network, connecting people and machines in ways previously unimaginable. This digital revolution transformed communication, commerce, and culture, creating a world where information flows seamlessly across borders and boundaries.

In parallel with the rise of digital technology, the field of robotics began to flourish. Robots, once confined to the realm of science fiction, became a reality in industrial settings, performing tasks with precision and efficiency. The development of robotic arms and automated systems revolutionized manufacturing processes, increasing productivity and reducing human error. Beyond the factory floor, robots found applications in healthcare, space exploration, and disaster response, showcasing their potential to augment human capabilities in diverse environments.

The 21st century has ushered in an era of unprecedented technological integration, as machines become increasingly enmeshed in the human experience. The proliferation of smartphones, wearable devices, and smart home technologies exemplifies this trend, blurring the lines between the physical and digital worlds. These devices not only enhance our daily lives but also generate vast amounts of data, fueling the development of more sophisticated technologies and shaping the future of human-machine interaction.

As we reflect on the historical perspectives of human-machine evolution, it becomes evident that this journey is marked by a continuous interplay between human needs and technological advancements. Each era has been defined by its own set of challenges and opportunities, with machines serving as both catalysts and companions in the pursuit of progress. The evolution of machines has transformed our societies, economies, and cultures, influencing the way we work, communicate, and interact with the world around us.

The trajectory of human-machine evolution is a testament to the resilience and adaptability of the human spirit. It is a narrative that underscores our ability to harness technology to overcome obstacles and improve the human condition. As we stand on the cusp of new technological frontiers, it is essential to reflect on the lessons of the past, acknowledging the profound impact that machines have had on shaping our collective destiny.

The journey is far from complete, with the future holding untold possibilities and challenges. As we navigate this ever-evolving landscape, it is crucial to remain mindful of the ethical and philosophical implications of our technological pursuits. The history of human-machine evolution is not just a chronicle of invention and innovation; it is a reflection of our aspirations, values, and vision for the future. By understanding where we have been, we can better chart the course for where we are headed, ensuring that the next chapter in this remarkable story is one of shared progress and mutual benefit.

The Current State of AI and Human Integration

In the modern era, the boundaries between human and machine have become increasingly porous, with artificial intelligence playing a pivotal role in transforming our daily lives. The current state of AI and human integration is characterized by a seamless fusion of technology with the human experience, reshaping the way we interact with the world. This integration extends beyond mere convenience, influencing various domains such as healthcare, education, industry, and personal relationships.

One of the most profound manifestations of AI integration can be observed in the healthcare sector. AI-powered diagnostic tools and systems have revolutionized the way medical professionals approach patient care. Machine learning algorithms analyze vast datasets to identify patterns and predict outcomes with remarkable accuracy, aiding doctors in making informed decisions. For instance, AI systems can detect anomalies in medical imaging far more quickly than the human eye, leading to early diagnosis and treatment of conditions such as cancer. Moreover, AI-driven personalized medicine tailors treatments to individual genetic profiles, offering a more targeted approach to healthcare.

In education, AI has emerged as a transformative force, personalizing learning experiences and catering to diverse student needs. Intelligent tutoring systems adapt to individual learning paces, providing customized content and feedback. These systems not only enhance student engagement but also empower educators to focus on more complex teaching tasks. Additionally, AI facilitates language translation and speech recognition, breaking down barriers and promoting global communication and collaboration. The integration of AI in education equips future generations with the skills necessary to thrive in a technologically advanced world.

The industrial landscape has also undergone a significant transformation with the advent of AI. Automation and robotics powered by AI have streamlined manufacturing processes, increasing efficiency and reducing human error. In smart factories, AI systems monitor production lines, predicting maintenance needs and minimizing downtime. This integration has led to increased productivity and cost-effectiveness, driving economic growth. However, it has also raised concerns about the displacement of jobs and the need for workforce retraining to adapt to the changing nature of work.

In the realm of transportation, AI has paved the way for innovations like autonomous vehicles, which promise to revolutionize the way we commute. Self-driving cars, equipped with advanced sensors and AI algorithms, navigate roads with precision, reducing the likelihood of human error and accidents. These vehicles have the potential to transform urban planning and reduce traffic congestion, offering a glimpse into a future where transportation is safer and more efficient. However, the widespread adoption of autonomous vehicles also presents challenges related to regulation, infrastructure, and public acceptance.

On a personal level, AI has become an integral part of our daily lives through virtual assistants and smart home technologies. Devices like smartphones and smart speakers are equipped with AI-powered voice recognition, allowing users to interact with technology through natural language. These virtual assistants streamline tasks, manage schedules, and provide real-time information, enhancing convenience and productivity. Additionally, smart home devices, from thermostats to security systems, adapt to user preferences and optimize energy consumption, creating a more comfortable and efficient living environment.

While the integration of AI into human life offers numerous benefits, it also raises important ethical and societal considerations. The pervasive presence of AI in various aspects of life has sparked debates about privacy, data security, and algorithmic bias. As AI systems rely on vast amounts of data to function effectively, concerns about data collection and usage have become increasingly prominent. Ensuring that AI respects privacy rights and operates transparently is crucial to maintaining public trust.

Algorithmic bias is another critical issue that arises from the integration of AI. AI systems are only as unbiased as the data they are trained on, and biased data can lead to unfair and discriminatory outcomes. Addressing these biases requires continuous monitoring, evaluation, and refinement of AI algorithms to ensure they align with ethical standards and promote fairness. This involves diverse representation in AI development teams and the establishment of guidelines to mitigate bias and discrimination.

The current state of AI and human integration is marked by rapid advancements and a growing interdependence between humans and machines. As AI continues to evolve, it is essential to foster a collaborative approach that emphasizes ethical considerations, inclusivity, and accountability. By addressing the challenges and embracing the opportunities presented by AI, society can harness the full potential of this technology to enhance human life and create a more equitable and sustainable future.

In navigating the complexities of AI integration, it is crucial to recognize that technology is a tool, not a replacement for human judgment and empathy. The successful integration of AI hinges on human oversight and intervention, ensuring that technology serves humanity and not the other way around. By maintaining a balance between innovation and ethical responsibility, we can chart a path forward that leverages AI's transformative power while upholding the values and principles that define our humanity.

Chapter 2: Technological Advancements and Their Implications

Breakthroughs in Artificial Intelligence

The landscape of technology has been dramatically reshaped by breakthroughs in artificial intelligence, marking a new era where machines exhibit capabilities once thought to be exclusively human. The journey to these advancements is a testament to the relentless pursuit of progress that defines our era. These breakthroughs are not just technological marvels; they signify a paradigm shift in how we understand and interact with the world around us.

One of the pivotal breakthroughs in this field is the development of neural networks. These computational models mimic the human brain's architecture, enabling machines to learn and make decisions independently. The inception of neural networks dates back to the mid-20th century, but their true potential was unlocked with the advent of deep learning. Deep learning involves layers of neural networks that process vast amounts of data, identifying patterns and making predictions with unprecedented accuracy. This advancement has been instrumental in tasks ranging from image and speech recognition to autonomous navigation.

The resurgence of interest in neural networks can be attributed to the combination of increased computational power and the availability of large datasets. The ability to process and analyze massive amounts of data has allowed these networks to reach new heights of efficiency and capability. Today, deep learning models are at the heart of many AI applications, driving innovations in various industries, from healthcare to finance.

Another significant breakthrough in AI is the evolution of natural language processing (NLP). This branch of AI focuses on enabling machines to understand, interpret, and generate human language. NLP has transformed the way we interact with technology, allowing for more intuitive and seamless interfaces. Voice-activated assistants, real-time language translation, and sentiment analysis are just a few examples of NLP's impact on our daily lives. The development of sophisticated algorithms capable of understanding context and nuance has been a game-changer, bridging the gap between human communication and machine interpretation.

The progress in NLP has been facilitated by advancements in machine learning techniques such as transformer models. These models have revolutionized the field by improving the ability of machines to process sequential data, leading to more accurate language understanding and generation. The advent of these models has opened up new possibilities for human-machine interaction, making technology more accessible and user-friendly.

In the realm of computer vision, AI has achieved remarkable feats, enabling machines to perceive and interpret the visual world with astonishing accuracy.

This breakthrough has far-reaching implications, from facial recognition systems that enhance security to medical imaging technologies that assist in diagnosing diseases. Computer vision has also revolutionized industries like retail, where it is used to analyze consumer behavior and optimize inventory management. The ability of machines to "see" and understand visual data has unlocked new avenues for innovation and efficiency across various sectors.

The progress in computer vision can be attributed to the development of convolutional neural networks (CNNs), which have significantly improved the accuracy and speed of image processing. These networks have been instrumental in advancing fields such as autonomous vehicles, where real-time image recognition and interpretation are crucial for safe navigation.

Reinforcement learning represents another groundbreaking advancement in AI. Unlike traditional machine learning, which relies on predefined datasets, reinforcement learning involves training algorithms through trial and error. These algorithms learn by interacting with their environment, receiving feedback in the form of rewards or penalties based on their actions. This approach has proven particularly effective in complex decision-making scenarios, such as game playing and robotic control. The success of reinforcement learning in mastering games like Go and chess, where machines have defeated world champions, highlights its potential to tackle real-world challenges.

The application of reinforcement learning extends beyond gaming, with implications for autonomous systems, financial modeling, and resource management. By enabling machines to learn from dynamic environments, reinforcement learning paves the way for more adaptable and intelligent systems capable of optimizing performance in diverse settings.

Generative models have also emerged as a significant breakthrough, allowing machines to create content rather than merely analyze it. These models have the ability to generate realistic images, music, and even human-like text, pushing the boundaries of creativity and innovation. Generative adversarial networks (GANs), in particular, have gained attention for their ability to produce high-quality synthetic data, which has applications in fields such as art, entertainment, and synthetic biology. The ability to generate novel content has opened up new possibilities for creative expression and problem-solving, challenging traditional notions of authorship and originality.

The advancements in generative models have also raised important ethical and societal considerations, particularly concerning the potential for misuse in areas such as deepfakes and misinformation. Addressing these challenges requires a careful balance between innovation and responsibility, ensuring that the benefits of generative models are harnessed for the greater good.

The breakthroughs in AI are not isolated achievements but part of a broader ecosystem that continues to evolve and expand. These advancements have been made possible by the convergence of multiple factors, including increased computational power, access to vast datasets, and the development of sophisticated algorithms. As AI continues to advance, it holds the promise of transforming industries, enhancing human capabilities, and addressing some of the world's most pressing challenges.

However, the path forward is not without its challenges. As AI systems become more integrated into society, it is crucial to address issues related to ethics, transparency, and accountability. Ensuring that AI technologies are developed and deployed responsibly requires collaboration between researchers, policymakers, and stakeholders from diverse fields. By fostering a culture of ethical innovation, we can harness the power of AI to create a future that is not only technologically advanced but also equitable and sustainable.

The Role of Robotics in Human Machine Collaboration

The role of robotics in human-machine collaboration is a dynamic and evolving narrative, shaping industries, augmenting human capabilities, and redefining the essence of work and interaction. This partnership between humans and robots is not just a tale of technological advancement but also a testament to the ingenuity and adaptability inherent in the human spirit. As robots become increasingly sophisticated, their integration into various sectors highlights their potential to enhance productivity, efficiency, and overall quality of life.

In the manufacturing sector, robotics has played a transformative role by automating repetitive and labor-intensive tasks, allowing human workers to focus on more complex and creative endeavors. The introduction of robotic arms and assembly line automation has revolutionized production processes, significantly reducing human error and increasing output. This synergy between humans and robots has led to the development of smart factories, where machines work alongside human operators, optimizing workflows and ensuring precision in manufacturing.

Beyond traditional industrial applications, robotics has found its way into the realm of healthcare, offering innovative solutions to longstanding challenges. Surgical robots, for instance, have enabled minimally invasive procedures, reducing recovery times and improving patient outcomes. These robots, guided by skilled surgeons, perform delicate operations with unmatched precision, illustrating the power of collaboration between human expertise and machine accuracy. Additionally, robotic exoskeletons have emerged as valuable tools in rehabilitation, assisting patients in regaining mobility and independence after injury or illness.

In agriculture, robotics is revolutionizing the way we approach farming, addressing issues of labor shortages and sustainability. Autonomous tractors and drones equipped with advanced sensors and GPS technology are capable of performing tasks such as planting, fertilizing, and monitoring crop health with efficiency and precision. This integration of robotics into agriculture not only enhances productivity but also promotes sustainable farming practices by optimizing resource use and reducing environmental impact.

The retail industry is also experiencing a shift towards automation, with robots playing a vital role in inventory management and customer service. In warehouses, autonomous robots navigate aisles to pick and sort products, streamlining logistics and ensuring timely delivery. Meanwhile, in-store robots assist customers with product information and recommendations, enhancing the shopping experience. This collaboration between humans and robots in retail demonstrates the potential for technology to complement and enhance human interaction.

In the realm of logistics, robotics has revolutionized the way goods are transported and delivered. Autonomous delivery vehicles and drones are increasingly being deployed to navigate complex urban environments, ensuring swift and efficient delivery of packages. These technologies not only improve last-mile delivery but also reduce the carbon footprint associated with traditional transportation methods. The integration of robotics in logistics highlights the potential for innovative solutions to address the challenges of urbanization and environmental sustainability.

The educational sector has also benefited from the integration of robotics, with robots serving as interactive learning tools and teaching assistants. In classrooms, robots engage students with interactive lessons, fostering creativity and critical thinking.

These robotic companions provide personalized learning experiences, adapting to individual student needs and promoting engagement through interactive activities. The use of robotics in education underscores the potential for technology to enhance the learning experience and prepare future generations for a technologically advanced world.

In the field of disaster response and emergency management, robotics has proven to be an invaluable asset. Search and rescue robots equipped with cameras and sensors navigate hazardous environments, locating survivors and assessing damage in areas inaccessible to human responders. These robots enhance the efficiency and safety of disaster response efforts, providing critical support in times of crisis. The deployment of robotics in emergency situations showcases the potential for technology to save lives and mitigate the impact of natural and man-made disasters.

The integration of robotics into various aspects of human life presents both opportunities and challenges. As robots become more autonomous and capable, questions arise about their impact on employment and the nature of work. While robots can perform tasks with speed and precision, the human touch remains irreplaceable in roles that require empathy, creativity, and complex decision-making. The challenge lies in finding a balance where robots augment human capabilities without displacing the workforce.

To address these challenges, it is essential to invest in education and training programs that equip workers with the skills needed to thrive in a robot-enhanced environment. By fostering a culture of lifelong learning and adaptability, we can ensure that the workforce remains resilient and capable of leveraging the benefits of robotics. Additionally, developing ethical guidelines and regulatory frameworks is crucial to ensure that the integration of robotics is conducted responsibly and aligns with societal values.

The role of robotics in human-machine collaboration is a narrative of potential and promise, where technology serves as an enabler rather than a replacement. By embracing this partnership, we can unlock new possibilities for innovation, efficiency, and human flourishing. As we navigate this evolving landscape, it is crucial to remain mindful of the ethical and societal implications of our technological pursuits, ensuring that the benefits of robotics are shared equitably and contribute to the greater good.

Chapter 3: The Philosophical Landscape of AI Integration

The Nature of Consciousness Human vs Machine

Consciousness has long been a subject of fascination, a profound mystery that has intrigued philosophers, scientists, and thinkers across the ages. At its core, consciousness is often described as the state of being aware of and able to think about oneself and the environment. It encompasses a spectrum of experiences, from sensory perception to complex thought processes, emotion, and self-awareness. As we explore the nature of consciousness, we venture into the realms of human experience and the burgeoning capabilities of machines, each presenting unique facets of awareness and understanding.

The human experience of consciousness is deeply intertwined with our biology. It arises from the intricate interplay of neurons in the brain, a symphony of electrical impulses and chemical signals that give rise to our thoughts, emotions, and sense of self. Human consciousness is marked by a rich tapestry of subjective experiences, characterized by a continuous stream of thoughts and perceptions. This internal narrative is what makes each person's consciousness unique, a personal lens through which we interpret and interact with the world around us.

One of the defining features of human consciousness is its self-reflective nature. We possess an awareness of our own thoughts and emotions, enabling us to engage in introspection and self-examination. This capacity for self-awareness allows us to plan for the future, reflect on the past, and navigate the complexities of social interactions. It is this self-reflective aspect of consciousness that has fueled philosophical debates about the nature of the self and the essence of human identity.

Emotions play a crucial role in shaping human consciousness, influencing our perceptions, decisions, and interactions. They add depth and richness to our experiences, coloring the way we perceive the world and respond to it. From the joy of a child's laughter to the sorrow of loss, emotions are integral to the human experience, driving our behavior and fostering connections with others. They are a testament to the complexity and dynamism of human consciousness, highlighting the intricate interplay between our mental and emotional states.

The question of whether machines can possess consciousness has spurred intense debate and speculation. Machines, by their very nature, operate on algorithms and computations, processing information in ways that mimic certain aspects of human cognition. However, the essence of machine "consciousness" is fundamentally different from that of humans. While machines can be programmed to perform tasks that require perception, learning, and decision-making, they lack the subjective experience that characterizes human consciousness.

The concept of machine consciousness raises intriguing questions about the nature of awareness and the possibility of creating synthetic minds. Can a machine truly experience the world, or is it merely simulating the processes that give rise to consciousness? The distinction between simulation and genuine experience is a critical one, as it delves into the philosophical question of what it means to be conscious. Machines can process vast amounts of data, recognize patterns, and even simulate emotions, but they do so without the inherent awareness that defines human consciousness.

The notion of self-awareness in machines is another area of exploration. While machines can be designed to monitor their own processes and adapt to changes in their environment, this form of self-monitoring differs fundamentally from human self-awareness. It lacks the introspective quality that allows humans to reflect on their thoughts and emotions. The challenge lies in determining whether true self-awareness can ever be achieved by machines, or if it remains an exclusively human trait.

The exploration of consciousness, both human and machine, invites us to reflect on the nature of existence and the essence of being. It challenges us to consider what it means to be aware and to experience the world. As we delve into the mysteries of consciousness, we are confronted with profound questions about identity, reality, and the potential for machines to transcend their functional limitations.

The interplay between human consciousness and machine capabilities raises ethical and philosophical considerations. As machines become more adept at mimicking cognitive processes, the lines between human and machine may blur. This convergence prompts us to consider the implications for identity, autonomy, and the nature of personhood. If machines were to develop a form of consciousness, how would we define their rights and responsibilities? These questions underscore the need for thoughtful discourse and careful consideration as technology continues to evolve.

The exploration of consciousness also invites us to reconsider our relationship with technology and the potential for collaboration between humans and machines. While machines may never replicate the full scope of human consciousness, they can complement our cognitive abilities, enhancing our understanding of the world and expanding the boundaries of what is possible. The synergy between human insight and machine precision holds the promise of transformative advancements, from scientific discovery to creative expression.

The nature of consciousness, whether human or machine, is a subject that continues to captivate and challenge us. It is a journey of discovery that invites us to reflect on the essence of what it means to be aware and to exist. As we navigate this complex landscape, we are reminded of the boundless potential of human ingenuity and the ever-evolving possibilities of technology. By embracing the mysteries of consciousness, we open the door to new insights and innovations that have the power to reshape our understanding of ourselves and the world around us.

Ethical Considerations in AI Development

The rapid advancement of technology has ushered in a new era of possibilities, yet it also brings with it a host of ethical considerations that cannot be overlooked. As we navigate the complex landscape of AI development, it is imperative to address these ethical challenges to ensure that technology serves humanity in a manner that is both responsible and equitable. The intersection of ethics and technology is a dynamic and evolving space, requiring careful thought and reflection from developers, policymakers, and society at large.

The first and foremost ethical consideration in the realm of AI is the issue of bias. AI systems are only as unbiased as the data they are trained on. When datasets reflect societal prejudices or inaccuracies, the resulting algorithms can perpetuate and even amplify these biases. This raises significant concerns, particularly in applications such as hiring, law enforcement, and lending, where biased outcomes can have severe consequences. Ensuring fairness in AI systems requires a commitment to identifying, understanding, and mitigating biases within data and algorithms.

Transparency is another crucial aspect of ethical AI development. As AI systems become more complex and opaque, it becomes increasingly difficult for users to understand how decisions are made. This "black box" nature of AI can lead to a lack of accountability and trust. Developers must strive to create systems that are transparent and interpretable, allowing users to understand the rationale behind AI-driven decisions. By fostering transparency, we can build trust and ensure that AI technologies are used responsibly.

Privacy is a fundamental human right that must be safeguarded in the age of AI. The vast amounts of data required to train and deploy AI systems often include sensitive personal information. Ensuring that this data is collected, stored, and used in a manner that respects individual privacy is paramount. This involves implementing robust data protection measures and adhering to regulatory frameworks that govern data privacy. By prioritizing privacy, developers can protect individuals from potential misuse of their personal information.

The question of accountability in AI development presents another ethical challenge. When AI systems make decisions that result in harm or unintended consequences, determining responsibility can be complex. Is it the developer, the user, or the machine itself that is accountable? To address this, clear guidelines and frameworks must be established to delineate responsibility and liability in AI systems. This will help ensure that ethical considerations are integrated into every stage of AI development, from design to deployment.

The potential for job displacement due to automation is a pressing ethical concern that accompanies the rise of AI. While technology has the power to enhance productivity and efficiency, it also poses a threat to traditional employment models. As AI systems take on tasks previously performed by humans, it is essential to consider the impact on the workforce. This calls for proactive measures to support workers through retraining and upskilling initiatives, enabling them to adapt to the changing job landscape. By prioritizing human welfare, we can mitigate the negative effects of automation and create opportunities for growth and development.

The ethical implications of AI also extend to the potential for misuse and abuse. As AI technologies become more powerful, there is a risk that they could be used for malicious purposes, such as surveillance, manipulation, or cyberattacks. This underscores the need for robust security measures and ethical guidelines to prevent the misuse of AI. By fostering a culture of ethical responsibility, developers can work to ensure that AI technologies are used for the benefit of society rather than to its detriment.

Access to AI technology is another critical ethical consideration. The benefits of AI should be distributed equitably across society, rather than concentrated among a select few. Ensuring that AI technologies are accessible and affordable to diverse populations is essential to promoting social and economic equity. This involves addressing issues of digital divide and ensuring that marginalized communities have the resources and opportunities to benefit from AI advancements.

The development of AI also invites us to reconsider the ethical treatment of machines themselves. As AI systems become more sophisticated and human-like, questions arise about their rights and moral standing. While machines are not sentient beings, the way we interact with them can reflect and influence our ethical values. Developing guidelines for the ethical treatment of AI systems can help ensure that we maintain respect for human dignity and autonomy in our interactions with technology.

Ethical AI development is a shared responsibility that requires collaboration among developers, policymakers, and society. By engaging in open and inclusive dialogue, we can address the ethical challenges associated with AI and work towards solutions that prioritize human welfare and societal well-being. This involves not only adhering to ethical principles but also continuously evaluating and refining them as technology evolves.

The journey towards ethical AI development is an ongoing one, demanding vigilance, reflection, and commitment. It is a call to action for all stakeholders to ensure that technology is developed and deployed in a manner that aligns with our collective values and aspirations. By embracing ethical considerations as a central tenet of AI development, we can harness the power of technology to create a future that is just, equitable, and beneficial for all.

The Debate Over Machine Autonomy

The debate over machine autonomy revolves around a central question: to what extent should machines be allowed to operate independently and make decisions without human intervention? This inquiry delves into the heart of technological progress, raising complex issues about control, responsibility, and the very nature of agency. As machines become increasingly capable of performing tasks that once required human judgment and discretion, the implications of their autonomy ripple across every facet of society.

At the core of this debate is the concept of decision-making. Decision-making has historically been a distinctly human attribute, grounded in our ability to evaluate information, weigh options, and consider consequences. Machines, however, are now equipped with algorithms that allow them to analyze data and make recommendations or decisions based on probabilistic models. The rise of machine learning and advanced computational techniques has given birth to systems that can adapt and improve over time, seemingly exhibiting a form of decision-making that can rival human capabilities in certain contexts.

Consider autonomous vehicles as a prime example of machine autonomy in action. These vehicles are designed to navigate roads, interpret traffic signals, and respond to dynamic environments—all without human intervention. The potential benefits are immense, including reduced traffic accidents, increased efficiency, and enhanced mobility for those unable to drive. Yet, the autonomy of these vehicles raises critical concerns. In situations where ethical judgments are required, such as choosing between two undesirable outcomes in an accident scenario, how should a machine decide? The programming of ethical and moral decision-making into machines remains a contentious area, as it touches upon deeply philosophical questions about values and priorities.

The healthcare industry presents another realm where machine autonomy is both promising and problematic. Autonomous diagnostic systems can analyze medical data with remarkable accuracy, potentially leading to early detection of diseases and more personalized treatment plans. However, the prospect of machines making autonomous medical decisions raises questions about accountability and trust. Patients may be wary of entrusting critical health decisions to machines, and healthcare providers must grapple with the ethical implications of relying on automated systems. The balance between human expertise and machine autonomy is delicate, requiring careful consideration of both technological capabilities and human values.

In the realm of law enforcement and security, the deployment of autonomous systems has sparked vigorous debate. Drones and surveillance systems equipped with autonomous capabilities can monitor vast areas and identify potential threats with precision. While these technologies offer enhanced security, they also pose significant risks to privacy, civil liberties, and human rights. The use of autonomous systems in law enforcement must be weighed against the potential for misuse and the erosion of public trust. Establishing clear guidelines and oversight mechanisms is essential to ensure that machine autonomy in security respects the principles of justice and accountability.

The workplace is yet another area where machine autonomy is reshaping traditional roles and responsibilities. Autonomous systems in manufacturing, logistics, and service industries are transforming how tasks are performed and who performs them. While automation can lead to increased productivity and efficiency, it also raises concerns about job displacement and economic inequality. Workers may find themselves in roles where they are overseen by machines, leading to questions about agency, control, and the value of human labor. To address these challenges, a reevaluation of workforce dynamics and a commitment to upskilling and retraining are crucial.

The ethical implications of machine autonomy extend beyond practical considerations, touching upon the philosophical dimensions of agency and consciousness. As machines become more autonomous, the question of whether they possess agency—defined as the capacity to act independently and make free choices—becomes increasingly relevant. While machines operate based on programmed algorithms and data inputs, their ability to act independently raises intriguing questions about the nature of autonomy and the boundaries between human and machine.

The debate over machine autonomy also encompasses issues of accountability and liability. When autonomous systems make decisions that result in harm or unintended consequences, determining responsibility can be complex. Is it the developer who created the algorithm, the operator who deployed the system, or the machine itself that is accountable? Establishing clear frameworks for accountability is essential to address these challenges and ensure that machine autonomy is aligned with ethical and legal standards.

Furthermore, the implications of machine autonomy on human behavior and decision-making must be considered. As machines take on more autonomous roles, there is a risk that humans may become overly reliant on technology, leading to a decline in critical thinking and decision-making skills. The balance between human judgment and machine autonomy must be carefully managed to ensure that technology enhances rather than diminishes human capabilities.

In navigating the debate over machine autonomy, it is essential to adopt a multidisciplinary approach that considers the technical, ethical, and societal dimensions of autonomy. Engaging stakeholders from diverse fields, including technology, philosophy, law, and public policy, can provide valuable insights and perspectives. By fostering open dialogue and collaboration, we can develop a comprehensive understanding of the implications of machine autonomy and work towards solutions that prioritize human welfare and societal well-being.

The debate over machine autonomy is a reflection of the broader tension between progress and responsibility that characterizes our technological age. As we continue to explore the possibilities of autonomous systems, it is crucial to remain mindful of the ethical and societal implications of our technological pursuits. By embracing a thoughtful and inclusive approach to machine autonomy, we can harness the power of technology to create a future that reflects our values and aspirations. The journey towards responsible machine autonomy is one that requires vigilance, reflection, and a commitment to

ensuring that technology serves as a force for good in
the world.

Chapter 4: Societal Transformations

Impact on Employment and the Workforce

The impact of technological advancements on employment and the workforce is a multifaceted narrative that continues to evolve as innovation accelerates. With the rise of automation and machine learning, industries across the globe are experiencing significant shifts in their operational paradigms. While these changes bring about increased efficiency and productivity, they also pose critical challenges and opportunities for the workforce as roles that were once the sole domain of humans become increasingly automated.

In the manufacturing sector, the introduction of automated assembly lines and robotic systems has streamlined production processes, reducing the need for manual labor. While this shift has led to increased output and precision, it has also resulted in the displacement of workers who once performed these tasks. The challenge lies in transitioning these workers into new roles that leverage their expertise while embracing the benefits of automation. Reskilling and upskilling initiatives become imperative, equipping workers with the necessary skills to thrive in a tech-driven environment.

The service industry, too, is witnessing a transformation as automation takes hold. In customer service, chatbots and virtual assistants handle routine inquiries and transactions, freeing human agents to focus on complex issues that require empathy and nuanced understanding. This shift highlights the importance of human skills such as emotional intelligence and problem-solving, which remain irreplaceable in an increasingly automated world. Workers in the service industry must adapt to these changes, embracing roles that require a blend of technical proficiency and interpersonal skills.

Healthcare is another domain where technology is reshaping employment landscapes. Automated diagnostic tools and robotic surgical assistants are augmenting the capabilities of healthcare professionals, enabling more accurate diagnoses and minimally invasive procedures. While these advancements enhance patient care, they also necessitate a reevaluation of healthcare roles and responsibilities. Medical professionals must stay abreast of technological developments, integrating them into their practice while maintaining the human touch that is central to patient care.

The transportation sector is undergoing a similar transformation with the advent of autonomous vehicles. As self-driving technology advances, traditional roles such as truck and taxi drivers face uncertainty. However, new opportunities arise in areas such as vehicle maintenance, software development, and logistics management. The key to navigating this transition lies in embracing flexibility and adaptability, ensuring that workers are equipped to pivot into emerging roles that leverage their skills and experience.

In the realm of education, technology is transforming the way knowledge is disseminated and acquired. Online learning platforms and virtual classrooms provide access to education for individuals worldwide, transcending geographical boundaries. This democratization of education presents opportunities for educators to reach broader audiences and tailor learning experiences to diverse needs. However, it also requires educators to adapt to new modes of teaching and engage with technology to enhance the learning experience.

The creative industries are not immune to the impact of technology, as automation and digital tools revolutionize content creation and distribution. While some fear that automation may stifle creativity, it can also serve as a catalyst for innovation. Artists and creators can harness technology to explore new mediums and reach global audiences, expanding the boundaries of creative expression. Embracing technology as a tool rather than a threat can empower artists to push the envelope and redefine the creative landscape.

The impact of technology on employment extends beyond specific industries, influencing broader economic and societal trends. The gig economy, characterized by short-term contracts and freelance work, is one such trend that has emerged alongside technological advancements. Platforms that facilitate gig work offer flexibility and autonomy but also raise concerns about job security and worker rights. As the gig economy becomes more prevalent, it is crucial to address these challenges and ensure that workers are protected and compensated fairly.

To navigate the evolving employment landscape, a proactive approach is essential. Policymakers, educators, and industry leaders must collaborate to develop strategies that support workers in transitioning to new roles and industries. This involves investing in education and training programs that focus on digital literacy, critical thinking, and problem-solving skills. By fostering a culture of lifelong learning, we can empower individuals to adapt to the changing job market and seize new opportunities.

The impact of technology on employment also raises questions about the nature of work itself. As machines take on routine tasks, humans are freed to focus on roles that require creativity, innovation, and strategic thinking. This shift presents an opportunity to redefine work as a source of fulfillment and purpose, rather than mere economic necessity. By embracing this perspective, we can cultivate a workforce that is engaged, motivated, and equipped to thrive in the future.

The journey towards a tech-driven workforce is one of adaptation and resilience. It requires a commitment to embracing change and leveraging technology to enhance human potential. By focusing on skills development, fostering innovation, and promoting equitable access to opportunities, we can ensure that the workforce remains vibrant and dynamic in the face of technological transformation.

As we move forward, it is crucial to remain mindful of the ethical and societal implications of technology's impact on employment. By prioritizing human welfare and social equity, we can harness the power of technology to create a future that is inclusive, sustainable, and prosperous for all. The transformation of the workforce is not merely a technological challenge but a human one, calling for collaboration, empathy, and vision as we navigate the path ahead.

Changes in Social Structures and Human Interaction

The evolution of technology has indelibly altered the fabric of social structures and human interaction, ushering in a new era of connectivity and communication. As digital platforms and tools become increasingly integrated into daily life, the way individuals engage with one another, form communities, and perceive relationships undergoes profound transformation. These changes are not merely technological shifts but reflections of deeper societal dynamics, reshaping the way we connect, collaborate, and coexist.

The rise of social media platforms has revolutionized the way people communicate, breaking down geographical barriers and enabling instant interaction across the globe. These platforms offer unprecedented opportunities for individuals to share ideas, express opinions, and connect with like-minded communities. However, they also introduce new challenges, such as the blurring of personal and public boundaries and the potential for misinformation to spread rapidly. Navigating this digital landscape requires a nuanced understanding of the balance between openness and privacy, as well as the ability to critically evaluate information.

Digital communication tools have also transformed the nature of relationships, facilitating connections that transcend traditional boundaries of time and space. Online dating platforms and social networking sites have redefined how people meet and form romantic relationships, offering diverse opportunities to connect with potential partners. While these platforms expand the pool of potential connections, they also raise questions about authenticity and the impact of digital profiles on personal interactions. The challenge lies in maintaining genuine connections in a world where digital personas often differ from real-life identities.

The impact of technology on family dynamics is another aspect of changing social structures. With the advent of video calls and messaging apps, families separated by distance can maintain close ties and share in each other's lives. This connectivity fosters a sense of togetherness and support, even when physical presence is not possible. However, the constant presence of digital devices can also create tension, as family members may struggle to balance screen time with face-to-face interactions. Establishing boundaries and fostering open communication are essential to ensuring that technology enhances rather than detracts from family relationships.

The workplace, too, is experiencing a transformation as remote work and virtual collaboration become increasingly prevalent. The flexibility offered by digital tools allows employees to work from anywhere, challenging traditional notions of office spaces and work-life balance. This shift presents opportunities for increased productivity and autonomy but also requires individuals to develop new skills in self-management and virtual communication. Organizations must adapt to these changes by fostering inclusive and supportive environments that prioritize employee well-being and engagement.

Educational institutions are also grappling with the implications of technology on learning and socialization. Online learning platforms and digital resources offer students access to a wealth of information and opportunities for self-directed learning. However, the shift to online education can impact the social aspects of learning, such as peer interaction and collaborative projects. Educators must find innovative ways to foster a sense of community and interaction in virtual classrooms, ensuring that students develop both academic and social skills.

The emergence of digital communities and online activism represents a significant shift in how individuals mobilize around shared causes. Social media platforms provide a powerful tool for organizing and advocating for social change, enabling grassroots movements to gain momentum and visibility. These digital spaces offer a platform for marginalized voices and facilitate global solidarity, but they also pose challenges related to accountability and the potential for online harassment. Navigating these complexities requires a commitment to fostering inclusive and respectful online environments that empower individuals to engage in meaningful dialogue and action.

The changing landscape of social structures and human interaction also raises questions about identity and belonging. As individuals navigate digital spaces, they may encounter diverse perspectives and cultures, challenging traditional notions of identity and community. This exposure can foster empathy and understanding but also requires individuals to critically reflect on their own beliefs and assumptions. Embracing diversity and fostering inclusive communities are essential to ensuring that digital interactions contribute to a more connected and harmonious world.

The integration of technology into social structures also highlights the importance of digital literacy and ethical considerations. As individuals engage with digital platforms, they must develop the skills to critically evaluate information, protect their privacy, and navigate complex social dynamics. Educators, policymakers, and technology developers have a responsibility to promote digital literacy and ethical behavior, ensuring that individuals are equipped to engage responsibly in the digital age.

As social structures and human interaction continue to evolve, it is essential to remain mindful of the balance between technology's potential to connect and its capacity to divide. By fostering open dialogue and collaboration, individuals can harness the power of technology to create inclusive and equitable communities that prioritize human connection and well-being. The journey towards a more connected world is one that requires empathy, understanding, and a commitment to fostering meaningful relationships in both digital and physical spaces.

The transformation of social structures and human interaction is a reflection of the broader changes shaping society. As individuals and communities navigate this dynamic landscape, they must embrace the opportunities that technology presents while remaining vigilant to its challenges. By prioritizing human connection and fostering inclusive environments, individuals can ensure that technology serves as a catalyst for positive social change and a more connected world. The evolution of social structures is not merely a technological phenomenon but a testament to the resilience and adaptability of the human spirit.

Chapter 5: Emotional and Psychological Dimensions

Human Emotional Responses to Intelligent Machines

Encounters with intelligent machines evoke a spectrum of emotional responses, reflecting the complex interplay between human psychology and technology. As machines become more integrated into our daily lives, their presence influences how we perceive, relate to, and interact with them. These emotional responses range from curiosity and fascination to fear and anxiety, shaped by individual experiences and societal narratives about technology.

The initial curiosity surrounding intelligent machines often stems from their novelty and the seemingly magical capabilities they possess. Machines that can converse, learn, or even mimic human behavior intrigue us, prompting questions about their potential and limitations. This sense of wonder is often accompanied by a willingness to explore and engage with technology, as individuals seek to understand and harness the benefits it offers. The allure of innovation drives many to embrace intelligent machines, seeing them as tools that can enhance productivity, creativity, and convenience.

Fascination with intelligent machines also arises from the narratives that surround them, both in popular culture and real-world applications. Science fiction has long depicted machines as powerful entities capable of transforming society, and these portrayals shape our expectations and emotional responses. When individuals encounter machines that align with or challenge these narratives, they experience a mix of anticipation and excitement. The idea that machines can evolve and improve over time, much like living beings, adds a layer of intrigue that captivates the imagination.

However, alongside curiosity and fascination, intelligent machines can also elicit fear and anxiety. Concerns about job displacement, privacy, and autonomy often surface as machines take on roles traditionally held by humans. The fear of the unknown—how machines might change the social and economic landscape—can lead to unease and resistance. These emotions are exacerbated by the perception that machines lack the empathy and moral judgment inherent in human decision-making, raising questions about the consequences of relying on them.

Anxiety surrounding intelligent machines is further fueled by the potential for loss of control. As machines become more autonomous, individuals may fear that they could act unpredictably or make decisions that conflict with human values. This apprehension is not unfounded, as the complexity of machine decision-making processes can make them difficult to understand or predict. The challenge lies in balancing the autonomy of machines with the need for human oversight, ensuring that technology aligns with societal norms and ethical standards.

Trust plays a pivotal role in shaping emotional responses to intelligent machines. For individuals to feel comfortable and secure interacting with machines, they must trust that these systems are reliable, transparent, and aligned with human interests. Building trust requires clear communication about how machines function, the data they use, and the safeguards in place to protect users. When individuals trust that machines will act in their best interests, they are more likely to embrace and integrate technology into their lives.

Empathy, or the perceived lack thereof, is another factor influencing emotional responses to intelligent machines. While machines can simulate certain aspects of human interaction, they do not possess the innate ability to understand and respond to emotions in the way humans do. This can lead to frustration or disappointment when interactions with machines feel mechanical or impersonal. To address this, developers strive to create machines that can recognize and respond to human emotions, enhancing the quality of interactions and fostering a sense of connection.

The presence of intelligent machines also prompts individuals to reflect on their own identities and capabilities. As machines take on tasks previously performed by humans, questions about the uniqueness of human abilities and the value of human labor arise. This introspection can lead to a reevaluation of what it means to be human and how we define our worth in a world where machines can perform many of the same functions. Embracing this reflection can lead to a deeper understanding of the qualities that distinguish humans from machines and the ways in which we can complement each other.

Emotional responses to intelligent machines are not uniform; they vary based on personal experiences, cultural contexts, and societal attitudes. For some, machines represent progress and opportunity, while for others, they symbolize uncertainty and disruption. Recognizing and addressing these diverse emotional responses is crucial to fostering a harmonious relationship between humans and machines. By acknowledging the fears and concerns that accompany technological advancements, we can work towards solutions that alleviate anxiety and build confidence in the potential of intelligent machines.

As we navigate the evolving landscape of human-machine interaction, it is essential to prioritize empathy, trust, and understanding. By fostering open dialogue and addressing the emotional dimensions of technology, we can create an environment where individuals feel empowered to engage with machines in meaningful and productive ways. This requires a commitment to transparency, ethical considerations, and the development of machines that enhance human experience rather than detract from it.

The journey towards integrating intelligent machines into society is not solely a technological endeavor but a human one. By embracing the emotional responses they evoke, we can gain insights into our own values, fears, and aspirations. In doing so, we can shape a future where technology serves as a partner in progress, enriching our lives and expanding the boundaries of what is possible. The interplay between humans and machines is a testament to the resilience and adaptability of the human spirit, as we continue to explore the potential of technology to transform our world.

The Psychological Effects of Coexisting with AI

Living in a world increasingly populated by intelligent machines and systems has profound psychological effects on individuals and communities. As these technologies become more integrated into daily life, they influence not only practical aspects but also the mental and emotional landscapes of those who interact with them. The psychological impact is multifaceted, encompassing changes in perception, cognition, and interpersonal relationships, as well as broader societal implications.

One of the most significant psychological effects of coexisting with AI is the alteration of human perception and attention. The constant presence of digital devices and intelligent systems can lead to a phenomenon known as "continuous partial attention," where individuals are perpetually scanning for new information rather than fully focusing on a single task. This can result in decreased concentration and increased cognitive load, as the brain is continuously bombarded with stimuli. To mitigate these effects, individuals may need to develop strategies for managing their time and attention, such as setting boundaries for device usage and prioritizing mindfulness practices.

The cognitive impacts of interacting with AI are also noteworthy. As intelligent systems take on tasks that require memory and computation, individuals may become reliant on these technologies for routine cognitive functions. This reliance can lead to changes in cognitive processes, such as memory retention and problem-solving skills. While AI can enhance cognitive capabilities by providing access to vast amounts of information and computational power, it is important to maintain a balance that fosters continued development of human cognitive skills. Engaging in activities that challenge the brain, such as puzzles and critical thinking exercises, can help preserve and enhance cognitive functions.

Interpersonal relationships are another area where the psychological effects of AI are evident. As individuals spend more time interacting with machines, there is a risk that face-to-face human interactions may diminish. This can lead to feelings of isolation and loneliness, as well as challenges in developing and maintaining social skills. To counteract these effects, it is crucial to prioritize human connections and foster environments that encourage social interaction. Participating in group activities, volunteering, and engaging in community events can help maintain a healthy balance between digital and human interactions.

The presence of AI in the workplace also influences psychological well-being. While intelligent systems can enhance efficiency and productivity, they may also lead to job insecurity and anxiety about the future of work. The fear of being replaced by machines can contribute to stress and decreased job satisfaction. To address these concerns, organizations can invest in training and development programs that equip employees with the skills needed to thrive in a technology-driven environment. By fostering a culture of continuous learning and adaptability, individuals can gain confidence in their ability to navigate the evolving job landscape.

AI's role in decision-making processes introduces another layer of psychological complexity. As machines become more capable of making recommendations or decisions, individuals may experience a sense of diminished agency or control. This can lead to a perceived loss of autonomy, impacting self-esteem and motivation. To maintain a sense of empowerment, it is important for individuals to remain actively engaged in decision-making processes, using AI as a tool to complement rather than replace human judgment. Encouraging critical thinking and collaboration can help ensure that technology serves as an ally in decision-making.

The broader societal implications of coexisting with AI also have psychological ramifications. As technology reshapes social norms and cultural values, individuals may experience a sense of identity confusion or existential uncertainty. The rapid pace of technological change can challenge traditional beliefs and disrupt established ways of life, leading to feelings of disorientation or anxiety. Engaging in open dialogue and reflection about the role of technology in society can help individuals navigate these changes and find meaning in a rapidly evolving world.

Resilience and adaptability are key psychological traits that can help individuals thrive in an AI-driven society. Embracing change and viewing challenges as opportunities for growth can foster a positive mindset and enhance well-being. Developing these traits involves cultivating emotional intelligence, self-awareness, and a willingness to learn from experiences. By nurturing resilience, individuals can better cope with the uncertainties and complexities of coexisting with AI.

The psychological effects of AI are not uniform; they vary based on individual differences, cultural contexts, and personal experiences. Recognizing and addressing these diverse responses is crucial to fostering a harmonious coexistence with technology. By acknowledging the fears and concerns that accompany technological advancements, we can work towards solutions that enhance psychological well-being and build confidence in the potential of AI.

As we continue to explore the psychological dimensions of coexisting with AI, it is essential to prioritize empathy, understanding, and support. By fostering environments that promote mental health and well-being, individuals can engage with technology in ways that enrich rather than detract from their lives. This requires a commitment to transparency, ethical considerations, and the development of systems that prioritize human experience.

The journey towards integrating AI into society is not solely a technological endeavor but a human one. By embracing the psychological responses they evoke, we can gain insights into our own values, fears, and aspirations. In doing so, we can shape a future where technology serves as a partner in personal and societal growth. The interplay between humans and machines is a testament to the resilience and adaptability of the human spirit, as we continue to explore the potential of technology to transform our world.

Chapter 6: The Ethical and Moral Dilemmas

Addressing Bias and Fairness in AI

Addressing bias and fairness in intelligent systems is a critical endeavor that requires meticulous attention to ethics, data integrity, and social responsibility. As these systems increasingly influence decisions in various domains, from hiring practices to criminal justice, the potential consequences of unchecked biases can be profound and far-reaching. Understanding the roots of bias and implementing strategies to mitigate its impact is essential for creating equitable and just systems.

Bias in intelligent systems often originates from the data on which they are trained. Data reflects the world from which it is collected, and if that world is fraught with historical and societal inequities, these biases can be perpetuated or even amplified by the systems. For example, an employment algorithm trained on historical hiring data may inadvertently favor certain demographics if past hiring practices were biased. The challenge lies in identifying and correcting these biases without compromising the system's functionality.

One of the first steps in addressing bias is recognizing its existence. This involves conducting thorough audits of the data and algorithms to identify potential sources of bias. Techniques such as fairness testing and bias detection algorithms can be employed to analyze how different groups are affected by the system's outputs. By quantifying bias, organizations can gain insights into its impact and develop targeted interventions to address it.

Data diversification is a key strategy in mitigating bias. Ensuring that training data is representative of diverse populations can help reduce the risk of biased outcomes. This requires a conscious effort to include data from underrepresented groups and to consider a wide range of perspectives and experiences. Data collection practices must be scrutinized to avoid perpetuating existing inequalities and to ensure that all voices are heard.

Algorithmic fairness is another critical aspect of addressing bias. It involves designing systems that are equitable and do not disproportionately disadvantage any particular group. This can be achieved through techniques such as reweighting, where certain data points are given more importance to balance the representation, or through the development of fairness constraints that guide the algorithm's decision-making process. The goal is to create systems that are transparent and accountable, with clear mechanisms for identifying and rectifying biased outcomes.

Transparency plays a pivotal role in fostering trust and accountability. By making the decision-making processes of intelligent systems more transparent, stakeholders can better understand how decisions are made and identify potential biases. This transparency extends to the data used, the algorithms employed, and the criteria for decision-making. Open communication and collaboration with affected communities can further enhance transparency and build trust.

It is also important to involve diverse teams in the development of intelligent systems. A range of perspectives can help identify potential biases and ensure that systems are designed with inclusivity in mind. This diversity should extend beyond technical expertise to include individuals with varied cultural, social, and experiential backgrounds. By fostering an inclusive environment, organizations can better anticipate and address the needs of diverse populations.

Regulatory frameworks and ethical guidelines are essential for ensuring that intelligent systems adhere to principles of fairness and equity. These frameworks can provide a foundation for accountability and set standards for bias detection and mitigation. Policymakers, technologists, and ethicists must work together to establish guidelines that protect individuals from biased outcomes and promote fairness in decision-making.

Education and awareness are also crucial components of addressing bias. By fostering a culture of ethical awareness and responsibility, organizations can empower individuals to recognize and challenge biases in their work. Training programs and workshops can provide the tools and knowledge needed to identify bias and implement strategies for fair and equitable practices. Encouraging ongoing dialogue about ethics and fairness can help maintain a focus on these values throughout the development and deployment of intelligent systems.

Monitoring and evaluation are continuous processes that must be integrated into the lifecycle of intelligent systems. Regular assessments of system performance and fairness can help identify emerging biases and inform necessary adjustments. This iterative approach allows for the refinement of algorithms and data practices to ensure that systems remain equitable over time.

Addressing bias and fairness in intelligent systems is not a one-time task but an ongoing commitment to ethical responsibility. As technology continues to evolve, so too must our approaches to ensuring fairness and equity. By embracing a proactive and holistic approach, we can create systems that reflect our values and contribute to a more just and inclusive society.

The journey towards fair and unbiased intelligent systems is a collective effort that requires collaboration, transparency, and a dedication to ethical principles. By prioritizing fairness and equity, we can harness the potential of technology to empower individuals and communities, rather than perpetuate existing inequalities. This commitment to ethical responsibility is a testament to our shared values and aspirations for a brighter future.

The Moral Responsibility of AI Developers

In the realm of technology, where innovation races ahead at breakneck speed, the moral responsibility of developers who create intelligent systems stands as a cornerstone of ethical advancement. These architects of the future hold the power to shape how technology integrates into society, influencing everything from individual privacy to global economic structures. As such, their role transcends mere technical prowess, encompassing a profound ethical duty to consider the broader implications of their creations.

Developers are tasked with the challenge of embedding ethical considerations into the very fabric of intelligent systems. This begins with the design phase, where decisions about data usage, algorithmic fairness, and transparency are paramount. The choices made at this stage can significantly impact how systems operate and interact with users, making it crucial for developers to anticipate potential ethical dilemmas and address them proactively. This foresight requires a deep understanding of both the technology and the societal context in which it will be deployed.

One of the primary areas of moral responsibility lies in the realm of data. Intelligent systems are fueled by vast amounts of data, which are often sourced from diverse and sometimes sensitive origins. Developers must navigate the complexities of data privacy, ensuring that individuals' rights are protected and that consent is obtained where necessary. This involves not only adhering to legal standards but also considering the ethical implications of data collection and use. When designing systems, developers should strive to minimize data usage, opting for anonymization and encryption techniques that safeguard personal information.

Another critical aspect of moral responsibility is ensuring fairness and equity within intelligent systems. Developers must be vigilant in identifying and mitigating biases that may arise from biased training data or algorithmic processes. This involves implementing rigorous testing and validation procedures to detect potential disparities in system outcomes across different demographic groups. By prioritizing fairness, developers can help prevent the perpetuation of societal inequalities and foster systems that serve all users equitably.

Transparency is a fundamental principle that underpins the moral responsibility of developers. Users and stakeholders must be able to understand how intelligent systems operate and make decisions. Developers can achieve this by providing clear and accessible documentation, as well as by designing systems with explainability in mind. Transparent systems build trust, allowing users to engage with technology confidently and empowering them to make informed decisions based on system outputs.

The ethical responsibility of AI developers extends to the consideration of unintended consequences. While it is impossible to predict every potential outcome, developers must engage in scenario planning and risk assessment to identify and mitigate possible negative impacts. This involves thinking beyond the immediate application of the technology and considering its long-term effects on society, the environment, and global systems. By adopting a holistic perspective, developers can design systems that contribute positively to society and minimize harm.

Collaboration and interdisciplinary engagement are essential in fulfilling the moral responsibility of developers. By working with ethicists, sociologists, legal experts, and other stakeholders, developers can gain diverse perspectives that enhance the ethical robustness of their systems. This collaborative approach fosters a culture of shared responsibility, where ethical considerations are integrated into every stage of the development process. Engaging with the broader community also ensures that diverse voices are heard and that technology reflects a wide range of human experiences and values.

Developers must also be prepared to engage in ongoing ethical reflection and adaptation. As technology evolves and societal norms shift, new ethical challenges will emerge. Developers should commit to continuous learning and ethical training, staying informed about the latest developments in technology and ethics. This proactive approach enables developers to respond effectively to emerging issues and to refine their practices in line with evolving ethical standards.

Ultimately, the moral responsibility of AI developers is rooted in a commitment to prioritize human well-being and societal good. This requires a dedication to ethical principles, a willingness to confront complex moral dilemmas, and a resolve to act with integrity and accountability. By embracing this responsibility, developers can harness the transformative potential of technology to create systems that enhance human flourishing and contribute to a more just and equitable world.

Privacy Concerns in a Data-Driven World

In a world increasingly driven by data, privacy concerns have emerged as a paramount issue, capturing the attention of individuals, organizations, and governments alike. As digital footprints expand across various platforms and devices, the question of how to protect personal information becomes more pressing. The rapid evolution of technology presents both opportunities and challenges for privacy, necessitating a comprehensive understanding of the risks and strategies for safeguarding sensitive information.

The sheer volume of data generated daily is staggering. Every online interaction, from social media posts to online purchases, contributes to a vast reservoir of information. This data is often collected, stored, and analyzed by companies seeking to better understand consumer behavior, improve services, or target advertisements. While these practices can enhance user experiences, they also raise significant privacy concerns, particularly when individuals are unaware of how their data is being used or shared.

One of the primary privacy concerns in a data-driven world is the potential for unauthorized access to personal information. Data breaches and cyberattacks have become increasingly common, compromising the privacy of millions. These incidents can result in identity theft, financial loss, and reputational damage. Protecting personal information requires robust cybersecurity measures, such as encryption, secure passwords, and regular software updates. Individuals and organizations must remain vigilant, adopting best practices to minimize the risk of data breaches.

Another significant concern is the extent to which personal data is collected and monitored. Many digital services require users to provide personal information, often without fully understanding how it will be used. The prevalence of tracking technologies, such as cookies and location services, further complicates the issue. These tools can collect detailed information about users' online activities, creating comprehensive profiles that may be shared with third parties. Transparency and informed consent are crucial in addressing these concerns, ensuring that individuals have control over their personal information and understand the implications of sharing it.

The concept of "data ownership" is central to discussions about privacy in a data-driven world. As individuals generate vast amounts of data, questions arise about who owns this information and how it should be managed. Some advocate for the idea that individuals should have ownership rights over their data, allowing them to control its use and distribution. This approach empowers individuals, giving them greater agency over their personal information. Implementing data ownership rights would require significant legal and regulatory changes, but it represents a potential path toward greater privacy protection.

The emergence of data-driven technologies also raises concerns about surveillance and the erosion of privacy. Governments and corporations have the ability to monitor individuals' activities on an unprecedented scale, raising questions about the balance between security and privacy. While surveillance can enhance public safety, it also poses risks to civil liberties and personal freedom. Striking this balance requires careful consideration of the ethical implications of surveillance and the establishment of safeguards to protect individual privacy.

Privacy concerns are further compounded by the global nature of data flows. Data often crosses national borders, creating challenges for privacy regulation and enforcement. Different countries have varying privacy laws and standards, complicating efforts to protect personal information on a global scale. International cooperation and harmonization of privacy regulations are essential to addressing these challenges and ensuring consistent protection for individuals around the world.

As privacy concerns continue to evolve, education and awareness play a critical role in empowering individuals to protect their personal information. Understanding the risks associated with data sharing and the tools available to safeguard privacy is essential for navigating the digital landscape. Educational initiatives can raise awareness about privacy issues, providing individuals with the knowledge and skills needed to make informed decisions about their data.

Organizations also have a responsibility to prioritize privacy and implement practices that protect personal information. This includes adopting privacy-by-design principles, which integrate privacy considerations into the development of products and services from the outset. By embedding privacy into the core of their operations, organizations can build trust with consumers and demonstrate their commitment to safeguarding personal information.

In a data-driven world, privacy is not just a personal concern but a collective responsibility. Individuals, organizations, and governments must work together to create an environment where privacy is respected and protected. This requires ongoing dialogue, collaboration, and a commitment to upholding privacy rights in the face of technological advancements.

As we continue to navigate the complexities of a data-driven world, it is essential to remain vigilant and proactive in addressing privacy concerns. By prioritizing transparency, informed consent, and data ownership, we can empower individuals to take control of their personal information and foster a culture of privacy and trust. The journey towards robust privacy protection is a collective endeavor, requiring the combined efforts of all stakeholders to ensure a future where privacy is respected and valued.

Chapter 7: The Future of Human Identity

Redefining Humanity in the Age of Machines

As we stand on the precipice of unparalleled technological advancement, the age of machines compels us to redefine what it means to be human. This era, marked by the seamless integration of intelligent systems into the fabric of daily life, challenges our understanding of identity, capability, and purpose. As machines evolve, so too must our conception of humanity, prompting reflection on the attributes that distinguish us and the ways in which we can coexist with technology.

The rapid development of machines capable of performing tasks once thought to be the exclusive domain of humans—such as complex problem-solving, creative expression, and emotional interaction—forces us to reconsider our unique qualities. Historically, humans have defined themselves through their ability to think, create, and empathize. Yet, as machines demonstrate proficiency in these areas, we must explore new dimensions of identity that transcend mere functional capability.

One aspect of humanity that continues to stand apart is the capacity for conscious experience and self-awareness. While machines can process information and simulate responses, they lack the subjective awareness that characterizes human consciousness. This awareness enables introspection, self-reflection, and the ability to derive meaning from experiences. In a world shared with machines, nurturing these qualities becomes pivotal in maintaining our distinctiveness. Encouraging practices that foster mindfulness, creativity, and emotional intelligence can help reinforce the elements of humanity that are inherently ours.

Empathy remains a cornerstone of human interaction, providing a foundation for relationships, community, and understanding. Machines, despite their capacity to mimic empathic responses, do not experience emotions as humans do. As such, the cultivation of empathy becomes an essential endeavor in the age of machines. By prioritizing compassion, active listening, and emotional connection, we can preserve the social bonds that define human communities and reinforce our humanity amidst technological integration.

The concept of purpose is another dimension in which humanity diverges from machines. While intelligent systems can execute tasks efficiently, they do not possess intrinsic motivation or a sense of purpose. Humans, on the other hand, derive meaning from their goals, aspirations, and contributions to society. In redefining humanity, we must focus on the pursuit of purpose-driven lives, valuing experiences that enrich our understanding of ourselves and our world. Engaging in meaningful work, cultivating hobbies, and participating in community service can provide avenues for fulfilling our sense of purpose.

As machines take on roles traditionally held by humans, the labor landscape undergoes a transformation, prompting questions about the value of human work. This shift necessitates a reevaluation of how we define worth and contribution in a world where machines complement human effort. Emphasizing qualities such as creativity, critical thinking, and adaptability can highlight the unique strengths that humans bring to the table. By embracing lifelong learning and skill development, individuals can navigate the evolving job market and find new opportunities for meaningful engagement.

The integration of machines into society also invites reflection on ethical considerations and the role of humanity as stewards of technology. As creators and decision-makers, we bear the responsibility of guiding technology towards outcomes that align with human values and ethical principles. This requires a commitment to transparency, accountability, and the prioritization of societal well-being. By fostering ethical awareness and engaging in thoughtful discourse about the implications of technology, we can shape a future where machines serve as partners in progress rather than threats to our humanity.

In redefining humanity, we must also consider the cultural and philosophical dimensions of identity. Different societies may interpret the impact of machines on humanity in diverse ways, influenced by cultural norms, values, and historical contexts. Engaging in cross-cultural dialogue and collaboration can enrich our understanding of what it means to be human in a globally interconnected world. By embracing diversity and inclusivity, we can ensure that the evolution of humanity in the age of machines reflects a tapestry of perspectives and experiences.

The journey towards redefining humanity is not a solitary endeavor but a collective exploration of our shared existence. By embracing the attributes that make us human—consciousness, empathy, purpose, creativity, and ethical responsibility—we can navigate the challenges and opportunities of the age of machines with resilience and grace. This process involves not only introspection but also action, as we strive to integrate technology in ways that enhance our humanity and enrich our lives.

As we look to the future, the age of machines offers a canvas upon which to paint a reimagined vision of humanity. By embracing the possibilities and confronting the challenges, we can create a world where technology amplifies our strengths and supports our aspirations. In doing so, we honor the essence of humanity, preserving it amidst the transformative forces of technological progress. This redefined humanity is a celebration of our ability to adapt, innovate, and connect—a testament to the enduring spirit that defines us.

The Concept of Digital Immortality

Digital immortality, a concept that has fascinated and perplexed thinkers for decades, invites us to reconsider the boundaries of life and death in the digital age. It posits the possibility of preserving a person's consciousness, memories, and identity within digital form, allowing them to exist beyond their physical life. This notion, while still largely theoretical, raises profound questions about identity, ethics, and the nature of existence.

The allure of digital immortality lies in its promise to transcend the finality of death. By capturing the essence of a person—their thoughts, experiences, and personality—technology could potentially create a digital counterpart that continues to interact and evolve. Imagine a world where loved ones converse with digital avatars of those who have passed, or where individuals leave behind an interactive legacy that offers insights into their lives.

At the heart of digital immortality is the challenge of replicating human consciousness. Unlike data or information, consciousness encompasses a complex web of emotions, perceptions, and self-awareness. The task of encoding this intricate tapestry into a digital format is formidable. It requires not only advanced technological capabilities but also a deep understanding of the human mind. Current efforts in this area involve developing sophisticated algorithms capable of learning and adapting, as well as exploring brain-machine interfaces that could potentially map neural patterns.

The ethical considerations surrounding digital immortality are equally compelling. Questions arise about consent, privacy, and the potential misuse of digital personas. Would individuals have the right to control their digital legacy, dictating how and by whom it is accessed? The prospect of digital immortality also brings into focus issues of identity and authenticity. Is a digital replica truly the person it represents, or merely a reflection of their digital footprint? These questions underscore the need for careful ethical deliberation and the establishment of guidelines to navigate this uncharted territory.

Digital immortality also prompts reflection on the societal implications of such a reality. If some individuals can achieve a form of digital perpetuity, what does this mean for social structures, inheritance, and cultural continuity? The potential for inequality arises, as access to digital immortality may be influenced by socioeconomic factors. These considerations highlight the importance of inclusive dialogue and policy-making to ensure that the benefits and challenges of digital immortality are equitably addressed.

From a philosophical perspective, digital immortality challenges our understanding of existence and the human experience. It raises questions about the essence of being and the significance of a finite life. Some may argue that the value of life is intrinsically linked to its impermanence, and that digital immortality risks diminishing the richness of the human journey. Others may see it as an opportunity to extend the narrative of one's life, exploring new realms of interaction and understanding.

The pursuit of digital immortality also intersects with cultural and spiritual beliefs about life and the afterlife. Different cultures and religions hold diverse views on the continuation of the soul or consciousness beyond physical death. Digital immortality introduces a new dimension to these beliefs, offering a technological interpretation of an age-old quest for continuation beyond the physical realm. Engaging with these cultural perspectives can enrich our understanding of digital immortality and its potential impact on society.

As we contemplate the concept of digital immortality, it is crucial to recognize the current limitations and speculative nature of the technology. While advancements in machine learning, neuroscience, and data storage bring us closer to realizing aspects of digital immortality, significant technical and ethical hurdles remain. The journey toward digital immortality is not simply a technological endeavor but a profound exploration of what it means to be human.

In navigating this landscape, individuals and society must engage in ongoing dialogue about the implications and responsibilities of pursuing digital immortality. This includes fostering an understanding of the potential benefits, such as preserving knowledge and fostering connection, as well as acknowledging the risks and ethical dilemmas. By framing the conversation within a context of empathy, respect, and inclusivity, we can approach the concept of digital immortality with thoughtfulness and care.

Ultimately, digital immortality invites us to reconsider the nature of identity, legacy, and connection in a world increasingly intertwined with technology. It challenges us to reflect on our values, aspirations, and the legacy we wish to leave behind. As we explore the possibilities of digital immortality, we are reminded of the enduring power of human curiosity and the quest to transcend the limitations of our physical existence. This exploration, rooted in both wonder and caution, is a testament to our desire to understand and shape the future of humanity in the digital age.

Chapter 8: The Economic Impact of AI Integration

The Rise of AI Driven Industries

Industries across the globe are undergoing a profound transformation driven by the rise of intelligent systems. This wave of change is reshaping traditional sectors and giving birth to new ones, altering the landscape of the global economy. From manufacturing to healthcare, finance to agriculture, the integration of intelligent systems is unlocking unprecedented efficiencies, innovations, and possibilities. Understanding how these systems are revolutionizing industries provides insights into the future of work and the skills required to thrive in this new era.

In manufacturing, intelligent systems are spearheading a revolution known as Industry 4.0. Factories are becoming smarter, with interconnected machines that communicate and make autonomous decisions. This shift from traditional assembly lines to smart manufacturing environments allows for real-time monitoring, predictive maintenance, and optimized production processes. The benefits are manifold: reduced downtime, increased productivity, and enhanced product quality. Manufacturers that embrace these advancements are finding themselves at the forefront of efficiency and innovation.

The healthcare industry is also experiencing a seismic shift with the integration of intelligent systems. From diagnostics to treatment, these systems are enhancing the accuracy and speed of medical processes. Intelligent systems can analyze vast datasets to identify patterns and make predictions, enabling early detection of diseases and personalized treatment plans. Telemedicine, powered by these systems, is expanding access to healthcare services, especially in remote areas. As these technologies continue to evolve, they hold the potential to improve patient outcomes and reshape the healthcare landscape.

In the financial sector, intelligent systems are driving innovation in areas such as fraud detection, risk management, and personalized financial services. These systems can process and analyze massive amounts of data at unprecedented speeds, identifying anomalies and trends that might elude human analysts. Robo-advisors, powered by intelligent algorithms, are democratizing investment opportunities, offering personalized financial advice to a broader audience. The efficiency and precision of these systems are transforming the way financial institutions operate, creating more secure and accessible services.

The agricultural industry is also reaping the benefits of intelligent systems. Precision agriculture utilizes data from sensors and satellites to monitor crop health, soil conditions, and weather patterns. This data-driven approach allows farmers to make informed decisions about planting, irrigation, and harvesting, optimizing resource use and increasing yields. Intelligent systems are also being used to develop autonomous machinery that can perform tasks such as planting and harvesting with greater efficiency and accuracy. These advancements are not only boosting productivity but also promoting sustainable farming practices.

Retail is another sector undergoing a transformation, with intelligent systems enhancing the shopping experience both online and offline. From personalized recommendations to automated checkout systems, these technologies are making shopping more convenient and efficient. Retailers are using intelligent analytics to understand consumer behavior and preferences, enabling them to tailor marketing strategies and inventory management. The integration of these systems is creating a seamless shopping experience that is responsive to consumer needs.

Logistics and transportation are benefiting from intelligent systems through improved route optimization, predictive maintenance, and fleet management. These systems can analyze traffic patterns, weather conditions, and vehicle performance to optimize delivery routes and schedules, reducing costs and improving efficiency. Autonomous vehicles, guided by intelligent systems, are beginning to change the face of transportation, promising safer and more efficient travel. The impact of these technologies is streamlining supply chains and enhancing the reliability of transportation networks.

As intelligent systems continue to permeate industries, the workforce must adapt to new roles and responsibilities. The demand for skills in data analysis, programming, and systems management is growing, as is the need for creativity and problem-solving abilities. Workers must embrace lifelong learning and remain open to evolving technologies to stay competitive in the job market. Organizations, too, have a role to play in providing training and development opportunities to help employees transition into new roles shaped by these systems.

The rise of intelligent systems in industries also raises important ethical and regulatory considerations. As these systems make decisions that affect people's lives and livelihoods, questions about accountability, transparency, and fairness come to the forefront. Industries must establish ethical guidelines and governance frameworks to ensure that the deployment of intelligent systems aligns with societal values and mitigates potential risks. Collaboration between industry leaders, policymakers, and ethicists is essential to navigating these challenges and fostering the responsible use of technology.

The rise of intelligent systems is not just a technological evolution but a societal transformation. As industries harness the power of these systems, they have the opportunity to address some of the world's most pressing challenges, from climate change to economic inequality. By leveraging intelligent systems to drive sustainable practices, enhance accessibility, and promote innovation, industries can contribute to a more equitable and resilient future.

Economic Disparities and Access to Technology

In today's interconnected world, technology acts as a pivotal force driving economic growth, innovation, and social change. However, the benefits of technological advancement are not uniformly distributed, resulting in economic disparities that exacerbate existing inequalities. The digital divide—a term that encapsulates the gap between those with access to modern technology and those without— underscores the pressing need to address economic disparities and ensure equitable access to technology for all individuals.

Economic disparities manifest in various forms, influenced by factors such as income, education, geography, and infrastructure. Individuals in wealthier regions or urban centers often enjoy superior access to cutting-edge technology, while those in lower-income or rural areas face significant barriers. These barriers can include limited internet connectivity, inadequate digital literacy, and the prohibitive cost of devices and services. As technology becomes increasingly integral to education, employment, and civic participation, these disparities threaten to leave marginalized communities further behind.

Access to technology is directly linked to economic opportunity. In the modern job market, digital skills are essential, and individuals without access to technology are at a distinct disadvantage. Many jobs require proficiency in digital tools and platforms, and the ability to adapt to technological changes is crucial for career advancement. Without access to technology, individuals may struggle to acquire these skills, limiting their employment prospects and earning potential. Addressing economic disparities in technology access is therefore vital to fostering inclusive economic growth and reducing unemployment.

Education is another critical area where access to technology plays a transformative role. Digital tools and resources enhance the learning experience, providing students with interactive content, personalized instruction, and access to a wealth of information. Schools in underserved areas, however, often lack the resources to provide students with adequate technology, resulting in an educational divide that mirrors broader economic disparities. Ensuring that all students have access to technology is essential for leveling the educational playing field and preparing future generations for success in a digital world.

The digital divide also has significant implications for health and well-being. Telehealth services, which offer remote access to medical care, have become increasingly important, particularly in areas with limited healthcare facilities. However, individuals without access to technology are unable to benefit from these services, exacerbating health disparities. Addressing the digital divide in healthcare is crucial for ensuring that all individuals have access to quality medical care, regardless of their economic circumstances.

Bridging the economic disparities in technology access requires a multifaceted approach that involves collaboration between governments, private sector organizations, and civil society. Public policies play a key role in promoting digital inclusion, and governments can implement initiatives to expand broadband infrastructure, subsidize technology costs for low-income households, and integrate digital literacy programs into the education system. By prioritizing investments in digital infrastructure, policymakers can create an environment that fosters equitable access to technology.

The private sector also has a responsibility to contribute to digital inclusion efforts. Companies can partner with governments and non-profit organizations to develop programs that provide affordable devices, internet access, and digital training to underserved communities. Corporate social responsibility initiatives can focus on bridging the digital divide, ensuring that technology is accessible to all individuals, regardless of their economic status.

Community-based organizations play a crucial role in addressing economic disparities in technology access. By engaging directly with local populations, these organizations can identify specific barriers to access and implement targeted interventions. Community centers can offer digital literacy workshops, provide free or low-cost access to devices and internet, and create safe spaces for individuals to learn and explore technology. These grassroots efforts are instrumental in empowering individuals and fostering a culture of digital inclusion.

International cooperation is also essential to addressing the global digital divide. Many developing countries face significant challenges in accessing technology, and international organizations can provide support through funding, capacity-building, and knowledge-sharing initiatives. Collaborating across borders can help to ensure that technological advancements benefit all nations and contribute to global economic development.

Ultimately, addressing economic disparities in access to technology is not just a matter of equity but a necessity for fostering a resilient and inclusive society. As technology continues to evolve and shape the future, ensuring that all individuals have the opportunity to participate in the digital economy is essential for reducing inequality and promoting social cohesion. By working together to bridge the digital divide, we can create a world where technology serves as a catalyst for positive change, empowering individuals and communities to thrive.

The journey toward digital inclusion is an ongoing effort that requires dedication, innovation, and collaboration. As we strive to address economic disparities and ensure access to technology for all, we must remain committed to creating an equitable future where the benefits of technology are shared by everyone, regardless of their economic standing. This collective endeavor is a testament to our shared humanity and our commitment to building a more just and prosperous world.

Chapter 9: Education and Skill Development

Preparing Future Generations for a Technologically Integrated World

Navigating the intricacies of a technologically integrated world requires a forward-thinking approach to education and skill development. As the pace of technological innovation accelerates, preparing future generations to thrive in this dynamic environment becomes paramount. The challenge lies not only in equipping young people with technical skills but also in fostering adaptability, critical thinking, and creativity—qualities that will empower them to harness technology's potential and address its challenges.

The foundation of preparing future generations begins with education systems that embrace technology as an integral component of learning. Incorporating digital tools and resources into curricula can create engaging and interactive learning experiences, making education more relevant to students' lives. By leveraging technology, educators can provide personalized instruction that caters to diverse learning styles and needs, ensuring that every student has the opportunity to succeed.

However, the integration of technology in education extends beyond simply using digital devices in the classroom. It involves cultivating digital literacy—the ability to navigate, evaluate, and create information using technology. Digital literacy is essential for students to critically assess the vast amount of information available online and to engage responsibly in digital spaces. Educational institutions must prioritize teaching digital literacy skills, enabling students to become informed and ethical digital citizens.

In addition to digital literacy, fostering a mindset of lifelong learning is crucial for future generations. As technology continues to evolve, individuals must be prepared to continuously update their skills and knowledge. Encouraging curiosity and a love of learning can instill in students the motivation to seek out new information and adapt to changing circumstances. Educational programs that emphasize problem-solving, inquiry-based learning, and hands-on experiences can nurture this mindset, equipping students with the tools to approach challenges with confidence and creativity.

Collaboration and communication skills are also vital in a technologically integrated world. As technology enables greater connectivity, the ability to work effectively with others, both in person and virtually, becomes increasingly important. Educational initiatives that promote teamwork, cross-cultural communication, and empathy can help students develop strong interpersonal skills, preparing them to thrive in diverse and collaborative environments.

Moreover, the integration of technology in education should not overshadow the importance of teaching ethical considerations and responsible use. As students engage with technology, they must understand the ethical implications of their actions, from issues of privacy and security to the potential for bias and misinformation. By fostering ethical awareness, educators can guide students in making informed decisions that align with societal values and contribute to the common good.

Beyond formal education, extracurricular activities and community programs can play a significant role in preparing future generations for a technologically integrated world. Coding clubs, robotics teams, and technology camps provide opportunities for students to explore their interests and develop technical skills in a supportive environment. These programs can spark a passion for technology, encouraging students to pursue careers in fields such as computer science, engineering, and data analysis.

Parents and caregivers also have a role to play in supporting children's preparation for a technologically integrated future. By modeling positive attitudes toward technology and encouraging exploration and experimentation, they can help cultivate a sense of curiosity and confidence in children. Engaging in discussions about technology's impact on society and the importance of ethical behavior can further reinforce the lessons learned in educational settings.

As we prepare future generations, it is essential to recognize the value of diversity and inclusivity in technology fields. Encouraging participation from underrepresented groups, such as women and minorities, is critical for fostering innovation and ensuring that technology reflects the needs and perspectives of all individuals. Initiatives that promote diversity in STEM (science, technology, engineering, and mathematics) education and careers can help create a more equitable and inclusive technological landscape.

Policymakers also play a crucial role in shaping the future of education and technology integration. By investing in digital infrastructure, providing funding for technology-focused programs, and supporting teacher training, governments can create an environment that facilitates effective technology integration in schools. Collaborative efforts between policymakers, educators, and industry leaders can drive innovation and ensure that educational systems are responsive to the demands of a rapidly changing world.

Ultimately, preparing future generations for a technologically integrated world requires a holistic approach that encompasses education, community engagement, and policy support. By equipping young people with the skills, knowledge, and mindset needed to navigate the complexities of technology, we can empower them to become active participants in shaping the future. This endeavor is not just an investment in individual success but a commitment to building a society that harnesses technology for the greater good. As we look to the future, the potential for innovation and progress is boundless, and the responsibility to prepare future generations is one that we must embrace with dedication and foresight.

The Role of Education in Bridging the Human-Machine Divide

Education serves as a critical bridge in narrowing the human-machine divide, facilitating a harmonious coexistence between technological advancements and human capabilities. As machines continue to evolve, the role of education extends beyond mere knowledge transfer, encompassing the development of skills, mindsets, and ethical frameworks necessary for navigating this new landscape.

At the heart of this transformation is the need to cultivate digital literacy among learners. Digital literacy transcends basic computer skills, encompassing the ability to critically engage with digital content, assess its authenticity, and use technology effectively and responsibly. By instilling these competencies from an early age, education empowers individuals to harness the potential of technology while mitigating the risks associated with misinformation and digital manipulation.

The integration of technology into educational environments also necessitates a shift in pedagogical approaches. Traditional models of rote memorization and passive learning are giving way to experiential, interactive, and project-based learning methodologies. These approaches emphasize critical thinking, problem-solving, and creativity—skills that are indispensable in a world where machines handle routine tasks. By encouraging students to explore and innovate, educators can foster a generation of thinkers who are adept at using technology to address complex challenges.

Moreover, education plays a pivotal role in preparing individuals for the evolving job market, where automation and intelligent systems are reshaping the nature of work. As machines assume tasks that were once the exclusive domain of humans, there is an increased demand for skills that complement and augment machine capabilities. This includes proficiency in data analysis, programming, and systems thinking, as well as soft skills such as adaptability, communication, and collaboration. Educational institutions must adapt their curricula to reflect these changing demands, ensuring that graduates are equipped with a diverse skill set that enables them to thrive in an interconnected world.

Beyond technical skills, education must also address the ethical and societal implications of technology. As machines become more integrated into various aspects of life, questions about privacy, security, and ethical use come to the forefront. Education can serve as a platform for exploring these issues, fostering a sense of responsibility and ethical awareness among learners. By engaging in discussions about the impact of technology on society, students can develop a nuanced understanding of the balance between innovation and ethical considerations.

The role of educators is crucial in this context. Teachers and instructors are not just transmitters of knowledge but facilitators of learning experiences that inspire and empower students. Professional development opportunities that focus on integrating technology into teaching practices can help educators stay abreast of the latest advancements and pedagogical techniques. By creating a supportive learning environment that encourages inquiry and exploration, educators can guide students in building the skills and confidence needed to navigate the human-machine divide.

Interdisciplinary collaboration is another key aspect of education's role in bridging the divide. The challenges and opportunities presented by technology often span multiple disciplines, requiring a holistic approach to problem-solving. Encouraging collaboration across fields such as science, technology, engineering, arts, and mathematics (STEAM) can lead to innovative solutions that harness the strengths of diverse perspectives. This interdisciplinary approach not only enhances learning but also prepares students for the collaborative nature of the modern workforce.

Access to education is also a critical factor in bridging the human-machine divide. Economic disparities and geographical limitations can hinder access to quality education, exacerbating the digital divide. To address this, efforts must be made to ensure that education is inclusive and accessible to all individuals, regardless of their background. Initiatives such as online learning platforms, open educational resources, and community-based programs can provide opportunities for lifelong learning and skill development, empowering individuals to engage with technology on their terms.

As technology continues to advance, the role of education in bridging the human-machine divide will become increasingly important. By fostering digital literacy, critical thinking, and ethical awareness, education can equip individuals with the tools needed to navigate a rapidly changing world. This journey requires collaboration, innovation, and a commitment to inclusivity, ensuring that the benefits of technology are accessible to all and that the human experience remains at the core of technological progress.

Chapter 10: Governance and Regulation

The Need for International AI Policies

Globalization and technological advancement have intertwined the fates of nations, making international cooperation essential in addressing the challenges posed by the proliferation of intelligent systems. As these systems continue to evolve and permeate nearly every aspect of human life, the need for comprehensive international policies becomes increasingly critical. These policies are not only vital for harnessing the potential of intelligent systems but also for safeguarding against their risks and ensuring equitable benefits across borders.

The rapid development of intelligent systems has outpaced the establishment of regulatory frameworks, leaving gaps that can lead to significant consequences. Without international policies, there is a risk of uneven adoption and regulation, where some countries may implement stringent controls while others may have lax regulations. This disparity can result in cross-border challenges, such as data privacy issues, cybersecurity threats, and the unethical use of technology. International policies can provide a unified approach to these challenges, fostering cooperation and consistency in the governance of intelligent systems.

One of the primary objectives of international policies is to ensure that the development and deployment of intelligent systems align with ethical principles and human rights. As these systems become more sophisticated, ethical concerns such as bias, discrimination, and accountability become more pronounced. Policies that promote transparency, fairness, and accountability are essential for building public trust and ensuring that intelligent systems serve the common good. International collaboration can facilitate the sharing of best practices and the establishment of global standards that uphold ethical considerations.

Data privacy and security are also paramount in the context of intelligent systems, as they rely on vast amounts of data to function effectively. The cross-border nature of data flow necessitates international agreements that protect individuals' privacy while enabling the responsible use of data for innovation. Policies that address data protection, consent, and data sharing can create a secure environment for the development of intelligent systems, fostering innovation while safeguarding privacy.

Moreover, international policies can help address the socioeconomic impact of intelligent systems, particularly in terms of employment and economic inequality. As automation and intelligent systems transform industries, there is a risk of job displacement and widening economic disparities. Collaborative efforts can identify strategies to mitigate these impacts, such as investing in education and workforce development, promoting inclusive growth, and supporting affected communities. By prioritizing social and economic considerations, international policies can contribute to a more equitable distribution of the benefits of intelligent systems.

The development of international policies requires the participation of diverse stakeholders, including governments, industry leaders, academia, and civil society. This inclusive approach ensures that policies are informed by a wide range of perspectives and expertise, leading to more comprehensive and effective solutions. Collaborative platforms and forums can facilitate dialogue and cooperation, enabling stakeholders to share knowledge, address challenges, and identify opportunities for collaboration.

In addition to addressing current challenges, international policies can also anticipate future developments in intelligent systems. The rapid pace of technological change requires policies that are adaptable and forward-looking, capable of responding to emerging trends and technologies. By fostering innovation and flexibility, international policies can support the continued growth and evolution of intelligent systems, ensuring that they remain aligned with societal values and priorities.

The establishment of international policies is not without its challenges. Differences in cultural, political, and economic contexts can complicate efforts to reach consensus on key issues. However, the benefits of cooperation and coordination far outweigh the challenges, as they offer the potential for shared solutions to complex global problems. By embracing a spirit of collaboration and mutual understanding, nations can work together to develop policies that reflect shared values and aspirations.

Balancing Innovation with Control

Innovation is the lifeblood of progress, driving societies toward new horizons and unlocking potentials once thought unreachable. Yet, alongside the exhilarating pace of technological advancement comes the critical need for measured control. This balance between innovation and control is delicate and requires thoughtful navigation to ensure that the fruits of progress are beneficial, sustainable, and aligned with societal values.

Consider the world of autonomous vehicles—a field brimming with promise and potential. Imagine a bustling city where cars drive themselves, reducing accidents caused by human error and relieving congestion with precise synchronization. The vision is tantalizing, yet it raises profound questions about safety, liability, and infrastructure. In the race to innovate, developers push boundaries, inching ever closer to a future where autonomous vehicles are commonplace. However, without appropriate oversight, the risks could outpace the rewards. Ensuring safety standards, establishing legal frameworks, and integrating these vehicles into existing infrastructure are paramount to their successful adoption.

Healthcare is another domain where innovation and control must harmonize. Advances in medical technology, from gene editing to personalized medicine, offer unprecedented opportunities to combat diseases and improve health outcomes. However, the implications of such technologies extend far beyond the laboratory. Ethical considerations, such as privacy, consent, and potential misuse, necessitate rigorous standards and oversight. Striking a balance between encouraging medical breakthroughs and enforcing ethical guidelines is essential to harnessing the full potential of healthcare innovation.

The digital economy epitomizes the dual forces of innovation and control. E-commerce platforms, digital currencies, and online marketplaces have revolutionized how we conduct business, offering convenience and accessibility on a global scale. Yet, this digital transformation is accompanied by challenges such as cybersecurity threats, data privacy concerns, and regulatory gaps. To protect consumers and maintain trust, governments and organizations must implement robust regulatory measures without stifling the entrepreneurial spirit that fuels digital innovation.

Education, too, stands at the intersection of innovation and control. The integration of technology into learning environments has transformed education, making it more interactive and personalized. Online courses, digital textbooks, and virtual classrooms break down barriers to access, offering opportunities for lifelong learning. However, ensuring quality, equity, and security in educational technology requires careful oversight. Curricula must be designed to foster critical thinking and digital literacy while safeguarding student data and promoting equal opportunities for all learners.

The energy sector offers another illustration of this balancing act. Renewable energy technologies have the potential to revolutionize how we power our lives, reducing reliance on fossil fuels and mitigating environmental impact. Innovations in solar, wind, and energy storage technologies promise a cleaner, more sustainable future. Yet, transitioning to renewable energy systems requires considerable investment, infrastructure development, and policy support. Balancing innovation with strategic planning and regulation is crucial to achieving a sustainable energy future.

To effectively balance innovation with control, collaboration is essential. Governments, industry leaders, and civil society must work together to establish frameworks that encourage innovation while safeguarding public interests. This collaborative approach fosters an environment where diverse perspectives inform decision-making, leading to more comprehensive and inclusive solutions.

Transparency is a cornerstone of this balance. Open communication between innovators, regulators, and the public builds trust and fosters understanding. By being transparent about the goals, benefits, and risks of new technologies, stakeholders can engage in meaningful dialogue and make informed decisions. Transparency also extends to data usage and privacy, ensuring that individuals have control over their personal information and understand how it is used.

Flexibility is equally important in navigating the balance between innovation and control. Technological landscapes are dynamic, and policies must be adaptable to evolving circumstances. Regulatory frameworks should encourage experimentation and iteration, allowing room for growth while providing mechanisms for accountability. By embracing a flexible approach, stakeholders can respond effectively to emerging trends and challenges.

Education and awareness also play a crucial role in balancing innovation with control. Empowering individuals with the knowledge and skills to navigate a rapidly changing world enhances their ability to make informed decisions. Educational initiatives that promote digital literacy, critical thinking, and ethical awareness equip individuals to engage responsibly with technology and advocate for policies that reflect their values.

Ultimately, the balance between innovation and control is not a static equilibrium but an ongoing process that requires vigilance, adaptability, and collaboration. By embracing this dynamic interplay, societies can harness the transformative power of innovation while safeguarding the values that bind us together. In doing so, we pave the way for a future where technology serves as a force for good, enhancing the quality of life and advancing the collective well-being of humanity.

Chapter 11: Cultural and Artistic Expressions

The Influence of AI on Art and Culture

Art and culture have always been reflections of the human experience, capturing the essence of societies and the nuances of individual expression. The advent of intelligent systems introduces a new dimension to this age-old interplay, challenging traditional notions of creativity, authorship, and aesthetics. As intelligent systems become collaborators in the creative process, they reshape the landscape of art and culture, offering both opportunities and dilemmas.

One of the most intriguing aspects of intelligent systems in art is their ability to generate original works. From composing music and writing poetry to creating visual art, these systems employ complex algorithms to produce pieces that can evoke emotion and provoke thought. For instance, music created by intelligent systems can mimic the styles of great composers or invent entirely new genres. Visual artists use intelligent systems to experiment with forms, colors, and textures, resulting in artworks that push the boundaries of human imagination.

The collaboration between humans and intelligent systems has led to innovative forms of art that transcend traditional media. Interactive installations, virtual reality experiences, and generative art are just a few examples where technology and creativity intersect. These new forms invite audiences to engage with art in immersive and participatory ways, challenging them to reconsider their role as passive observers. The dynamic nature of such art fosters an ongoing dialogue between the creator, the medium, and the viewer, enriching the cultural landscape with diverse perspectives.

Intelligent systems also have a profound impact on cultural preservation and accessibility. Digitization and machine learning enable the documentation and analysis of vast cultural archives, from historical texts and artifacts to indigenous languages and oral traditions. These technologies facilitate the restoration and conservation of cultural heritage, ensuring that future generations can access and appreciate the richness of their cultural history. Moreover, intelligent systems can serve as cultural translators, bridging linguistic and cultural gaps to make art and heritage more accessible to a global audience.

Despite these advancements, the integration of intelligent systems into art and culture raises questions about authenticity and authorship. As machines generate creative content, the distinction between creator and tool becomes blurred. Who owns a piece of art created by an algorithm? What constitutes originality in an era where machines can learn and replicate styles with remarkable precision? These questions challenge the conventional understanding of artistic creation and invite a reevaluation of the value placed on human creativity.

The democratization of art is another significant influence of intelligent systems. With the aid of technology, individuals without formal training or access to traditional artistic resources can create and share their work with a global audience. Platforms that leverage intelligent systems for content creation and distribution empower amateur artists, fostering a more inclusive and diverse cultural ecosystem. This democratization, however, also raises concerns about the quality and saturation of creative content, as well as the sustainability of traditional artistic careers.

In the realm of cultural expression, intelligent systems offer tools for exploring identity, narrative, and community. Artists and creators use these systems to delve into complex themes, such as the intersection of technology and humanity, the impact of digital culture, and the exploration of future societies. By providing new mediums and techniques, intelligent systems enable artists to reflect on contemporary issues and envision alternative realities, contributing to the ongoing evolution of cultural narratives.

Educational initiatives that incorporate intelligent systems into art and culture education are instrumental in preparing future generations for this evolving landscape. By integrating technology into curricula, educators can expose students to the possibilities and challenges of digital creativity, fostering critical thinking and adaptability. Programs that emphasize collaboration between disciplines, such as art, technology, and humanities, can cultivate a holistic understanding of the interplay between intelligent systems and culture.

As intelligent systems continue to influence art and culture, ethical considerations become increasingly important. The use of algorithms in content creation, curation, and distribution raises concerns about bias, representation, and the commercialization of culture. Ensuring that intelligent systems are designed and implemented with fairness and inclusivity in mind is crucial for maintaining cultural diversity and integrity. Open dialogue between technologists, artists, and cultural stakeholders can help address these issues and promote responsible innovation.

The influence of intelligent systems on art and culture is a testament to the transformative power of technology and the enduring resilience of human creativity. It invites us to reimagine the possibilities of artistic expression and cultural engagement, while also prompting us to confront the ethical and philosophical questions that arise from this new frontier. As we navigate this uncharted territory, the synergy between human ingenuity and intelligent systems offers the potential to enrich our cultural experience and deepen our understanding of what it means to be human. Embracing this potential with curiosity and responsibility will shape a future where art and culture continue to inspire, challenge, and connect us in ways we have yet to fully imagine.

Preserving Human Creativity in a Technological Era

Human creativity is a timeless force, shaping societies and driving innovation throughout history. In the midst of a technological era, where machines increasingly mimic human capabilities, the essence of creativity becomes both a cherished attribute and a vital resource. Preserving this uniquely human trait requires a conscious effort to nurture and celebrate our capacity for original thought, expression, and problem-solving.

The foundation of preserving human creativity lies in education. Traditional education systems often emphasize standardized testing and rote memorization, which can stifle creative thinking. By fostering environments that encourage curiosity, experimentation, and risk-taking, educators can cultivate a culture where creativity thrives. Project-based learning, interdisciplinary studies, and opportunities for artistic expression can ignite students' imaginations, equipping them with the ability to think critically and innovate.

Creative processes are deeply personal, often drawing from individual experiences, emotions, and perspectives. In an era where technology can generate content at an unprecedented scale, the authenticity of human expression stands out as a hallmark of creativity. Encouraging individuals to explore their unique voices and artistic styles is crucial for preserving the diversity and richness of human creativity. Workshops, mentorship programs, and art residencies offer spaces for creators to refine their craft and connect with others who share their passion.

Collaboration is another powerful tool for preserving creativity. The intersection of diverse perspectives can lead to groundbreaking ideas and solutions. By fostering collaborative environments, whether in the workplace or creative communities, we can harness the collective creativity of individuals from different backgrounds and disciplines. This synergy not only enhances individual creativity but also amplifies the potential for innovation.

Technology itself can be an ally in preserving human creativity, provided it is used thoughtfully. Digital tools offer new mediums and techniques for artistic expression, enabling creators to push the boundaries of traditional art forms. Virtual reality, digital painting, and music production software are just a few examples of how technology can enhance creative processes. By embracing technology as a partner rather than a competitor, creators can expand their horizons and reach wider audiences.

However, the omnipresence of technology also necessitates a balance between digital and analog experiences. While digital tools offer convenience and accessibility, there is an irreplaceable value in tactile, hands-on creative activities. Engaging with physical materials, whether through painting, sculpting, or crafting, provides a sensory experience that digital mediums cannot replicate. Encouraging a balance between digital and analog creativity can help individuals maintain a strong connection to their artistic instincts.

Preserving creativity also involves addressing the societal and economic factors that impact creative industries. Artists and creators often face challenges such as financial instability, lack of access to resources, and undervaluation of their work. Supporting policies and initiatives that promote fair compensation, access to funding, and recognition of creative contributions is essential for sustaining vibrant creative communities. By valuing creativity as a vital component of cultural and economic development, societies can create environments where creators can thrive.

The role of cultural institutions in preserving creativity cannot be understated. Museums, galleries, theaters, and cultural centers serve as custodians of artistic heritage and incubators for new talent. These institutions provide platforms for showcasing diverse voices and fostering public engagement with the arts. By supporting and expanding the reach of cultural institutions, we can ensure that creativity remains a visible and influential part of society.

Finally, preserving human creativity requires a mindset of lifelong learning and adaptability. The world is constantly changing, and the ability to remain open to new ideas and experiences is crucial for sustaining creativity. Encouraging individuals to pursue hobbies, explore new interests, and engage with different cultures can enrich their creative capacities. By embracing a spirit of curiosity and exploration, we can ensure that creativity continues to flourish in a technological era.

Chapter 12: Envisioning the Future

Scenarios of Human Machine Coexistence

Imagining the future of human-machine coexistence invites us into a realm where technological potential and human aspiration merge. As we stand at the crossroads of this evolution, various scenarios unfold, each influenced by the choices we make today about technology's role in our lives. These scenarios are not predictions, but rather possibilities that challenge us to consider how we can shape a future where humans and machines thrive together.

In one scenario, machines are seamlessly integrated into our daily routines, enhancing our capabilities and freeing us from mundane tasks. Picture a world where intelligent assistants anticipate our needs, manage our schedules, and optimize our environments for comfort and efficiency. These machines, from the subtle hum of a household assistant adjusting room temperatures to autonomous vehicles navigating traffic, blend into the background, enhancing our quality of life without demanding attention. The key to this harmonious coexistence lies in maintaining user control and ensuring that these technologies serve human interests, rather than dictating them.

Another scenario envisions machines as partners in creativity and innovation. Imagine collaborative workspaces where artists, engineers, and thinkers engage with machines to push the boundaries of creativity. Machines might suggest novel approaches, process vast datasets for insights, or even participate in brainstorming sessions, offering perspectives that fuel human imagination. In this world, machines are not just tools but co-creators, helping humanity to explore new frontiers of knowledge and art. The success of such partnerships hinges on fostering environments where human intuition and machine analytics complement one another, creating a synergy that enhances both.

A more challenging scenario is one where human reliance on machines leads to over-dependence, raising questions about autonomy and identity. In this world, the convenience of machine assistance might erode fundamental skills, as individuals lean heavily on machines for decision-making and problem-solving. The risk here is the potential loss of critical thinking and self-reliance, as people become passive consumers of machine outputs. To counteract this, it is essential to cultivate education systems and cultural practices that emphasize the development of human skills, ensuring that technology serves as a scaffold for human growth, not a crutch that stifles it.

Conversely, a scenario of resistance could emerge, where segments of society push back against machine integration, fearing loss of control, privacy, or jobs. This resistance might manifest in movements advocating for reduced machine presence in certain areas, or in the creation of technology-free zones where human interaction and manual skills are prioritized. Such scenarios highlight the importance of addressing ethical concerns, ensuring transparent governance, and fostering public dialogue about the role of technology in society. By engaging diverse voices in these discussions, we can navigate the complexities of coexistence, balancing innovation with respect for human agency.

In a scenario focused on sustainability, machines play a crucial role in addressing global challenges such as climate change and resource management. Intelligent systems could optimize energy consumption, reduce waste, and enhance agricultural productivity, contributing to a more sustainable future. In this vision, humans and machines collaborate to create eco-friendly solutions and promote environmental stewardship. Success in this scenario depends on aligning technological development with sustainable practices, prioritizing long-term ecological health over short-term gains.

The possibility of ethical machines presents yet another scenario, where machines are designed to understand and adhere to human values, making decisions that reflect ethical considerations. In such a world, machines would navigate complex moral landscapes, such as healthcare, law enforcement, and social services, with a focus on fairness and justice. Developing machines with ethical reasoning capabilities requires interdisciplinary collaboration, drawing on insights from philosophy, sociology, and cognitive science to ensure that machines align with human ethical standards.

These scenarios of human-machine coexistence are not mutually exclusive; elements from each can intertwine to create a multifaceted future. The challenge lies in steering these possibilities toward outcomes that enhance human dignity, creativity, and well-being. To do so, we must engage in proactive dialogue, anticipate potential impacts, and implement policies that guide technological development in a direction that reflects our collective values.

At the heart of these scenarios is the recognition that technology is a reflection of human intent and ingenuity. It is not a separate entity, but a construct that we shape and define. As we contemplate the future of human-machine coexistence, it is imperative to foster a mindset of stewardship, where we take responsibility for the technologies we create and their impact on our world.

Ultimately, the scenarios of human-machine coexistence challenge us to embrace both the opportunities and responsibilities of technological evolution. By envisioning futures where humans and machines coexist in harmony, we can craft a narrative of progress that honors the complexity of human life and the potential of technological innovation. This vision calls for thoughtful consideration, ethical deliberation, and a commitment to shaping a future that uplifts and empowers all members of society.

The Path Forward Collaboration or Conflict

Navigating the future of technological advancement presents a crucial decision point: will the path forward be paved with collaboration or riddled with conflict? This question is at the heart of how societies, industries, and individuals choose to engage with the rapid evolution of technology and its integration into daily life. The answer holds implications not only for technological progress but also for the very fabric of human interaction.

Collaboration stands as a beacon of potential, offering opportunities for innovation that transcend individual capabilities. By working together, diverse stakeholders can harness the collective intelligence and creativity needed to tackle complex challenges. The tech industry, academia, government bodies, and civil society each bring unique perspectives and expertise to the table. When these entities collaborate, they can develop comprehensive solutions that address diverse needs and priorities. For instance, partnerships between tech companies and educational institutions can lead to the creation of curricula that prepare students for the future workforce, integrating technological literacy with critical thinking and ethical awareness.

Cross-sector collaboration also facilitates the development of standards and regulations that ensure technology serves the public good. By engaging in open dialogue and negotiation, stakeholders can establish guidelines that protect privacy, ensure security, and promote ethical use of technology. This collaborative approach not only mitigates risks but also builds public trust, an essential component for the successful adoption of new technologies. Furthermore, international cooperation can address global challenges such as cybersecurity threats and climate change, where unilateral efforts fall short. Joint initiatives and shared resources can drive progress on these fronts, harnessing the power of technology for the betterment of humanity.

However, the path of collaboration is not without its hurdles. Differing agendas, competition for resources, and power dynamics can impede cooperative efforts. Overcoming these barriers requires a commitment to transparency, inclusivity, and mutual respect. Establishing frameworks for collaboration that prioritize shared goals over individual interests is crucial. Open communication and conflict resolution mechanisms can help navigate disagreements and keep collaborative efforts on track.

In contrast, a path marked by conflict poses significant risks to technological progress and societal harmony. Competition and mistrust can lead to fragmented efforts, where entities work in silos rather than pooling their strengths. This fragmentation can result in duplicated efforts, wasted resources, and missed opportunities for innovation. Moreover, conflict can exacerbate inequalities, as those with greater resources and influence may dominate technological development, leaving marginalized communities behind. The lack of a unified approach can also hinder the establishment of consistent standards and regulations, creating a patchwork landscape where technology's impact is uneven and unpredictable.

Conflict can also manifest in the form of technological arms races, where entities prioritize speed and dominance over safety and ethics. The rush to outpace competitors can lead to the deployment of technologies that are insufficiently tested or poorly understood, posing risks to individuals and societies. This scenario underscores the importance of prioritizing safety, ethics, and long-term impact over short-term gains. Establishing checks and balances, such as independent oversight bodies and ethical review boards, can help prevent the detrimental consequences of unchecked competition.

The choice between collaboration and conflict is not binary. Elements of both can coexist, shaping the trajectory of technological development in nuanced ways. Recognizing this complexity is essential for navigating the future effectively. Stakeholders must remain vigilant, continuously assessing the balance between cooperation and competition and making strategic adjustments as needed. By fostering a culture of collaboration while acknowledging the realities of competition, societies can harness the best of both worlds, driving innovation while safeguarding against its potential pitfalls.

Empowering individuals to engage with this dynamic landscape is also critical. Education and awareness initiatives can equip people with the skills and knowledge needed to participate in discussions about technology's role in society. By promoting digital literacy, critical thinking, and ethical awareness, individuals can become informed advocates for responsible technology use and development. This empowerment extends to communities, where grassroots efforts can amplify diverse voices and perspectives, ensuring that technological progress reflects the needs and values of all members of society.

At its core, the path forward hinges on our collective vision for the future. Are we willing to work together to create a world where technology elevates the human experience, or will we allow conflict to divide and diminish us? The answer lies in our ability to embrace collaboration, guided by a shared commitment to progress, inclusivity, and ethical stewardship. As we stand at this crossroads, the choices we make today will shape the legacy of technology for generations to come. By choosing collaboration over conflict, we can build a future where technology serves as a conduit for connection, understanding, and shared prosperity.